EMERGING
SEXUAL
IDENTITIES

"In an era when so many conversations about sexuality feel hurried and anxious, this book is brilliantly patient. Yarhouse and Sadusky teach us how to slow down and ask better questions at the intersections of psychology, philosophy, and faith—questions that open dialogue with young people instead of shutting them down. This book will be a valuable resource for ministers, care providers, and parents alike."

—Gregory Coles, author of *Single, Gay, Christian* and *No Longer Strangers*

"For youth ministers and parents asking, 'What do young people really mean when they talk about their sexual or gender identities?'—this book is a gracious guide. With clarity and compassion, it takes you by the hand, unpacks the cultural conversation, and offers a thoughtful, wise path forward."

—Laurie Krieg, author and director of parent programs at The Center for Faith, Sexuality & Gender

"Many of us lack the experience to navigate the rapidly evolving perspectives on youth sexual identity. Yarhouse and Sadusky deepen our understanding beyond simplistic views, equipping us to respond with compassion and empathy. *Emerging Sexual Identities* offers grace-filled, biblically grounded, practical wisdom, helping us deepen the relationships with those we love when they need us most."

—Mark Matlock, founder of WisdomWorks; author of *Faith for the Curious*

"This is a very timely and important book. The authors' professional command of and experiential engagement with this subject matter will guide parents and parish/school staff to more informed, balanced, pastoral, and fruitful parenting and youth ministry."

—Most Rev. Thomas R. Zinkula, Archbishop of Dubuque

"Jesus bids us to read and judge wisely the signs of the times. In this book, Mark Yarhouse and Julia Sadusky do just that. They bring a keen attentiveness to emerging patterns and cultural trends, looking for what is of value in secular theory while holding firm to a Christian ethos. Christian ministers will find this a particularly helpful tool for understanding young people right where they are and for engaging their self-perception and journey of faith in creative ways."

—**Anna Carter**, cofounder and president, Eden Invitation

EMERGING SEXUAL IDENTITIES

NAVIGATING THE LANDSCAPE
with TODAY'S YOUTH

MARK YARHOUSE
AND JULIA SADUSKY

a division of Baker Publishing Group
Grand Rapids, Michigan

© 2025 by Mark A. Yarhouse and Julia A. Sadusky

Published by Brazos Press
a division of Baker Publishing Group
Grand Rapids, Michigan
BrazosPress.com

All rights reserved. No part of this publication may be reproduced, stored in a retrieval system, or transmitted in any form or by any means—for example, electronic, photocopy, recording—without the prior written permission of the publisher. The only exception is brief quotations in printed reviews.

Library of Congress Cataloging-in-Publication Data
Names: Yarhouse, Mark A., 1968– author. | Sadusky, Julia, author.
Title: Emerging sexual identities : navigating the landscape with today's youth / Mark Yarhouse and Julia Sadusky.
Description: Grand Rapids, Michigan : Brazos Press, a division of Baker Publishing Group, [2025] | Includes bibliographical references and index.
Identifiers: LCCN 2025015189 | ISBN 9781587436444 (paperback) | ISBN 9781493452231 (ebook)
Subjects: LCSH: Gender identity—Religious aspects—Christianity. | Sexual orientation—Religious aspects—Christianity. | Church work with transgender people. | Transgender people—Identity.
Classification: LCC BT708 .Y367 2025 | DDC 241/.66—dc23/eng/20250623
LC record available at https://lccn.loc.gov/2025015189

Scripture quotations are taken from the Holy Bible, New International Version®, NIV®. Copyright © 1973, 1978, 1984, 2011 by Biblica, Inc.® Used by permission of Zondervan. All rights reserved worldwide. www.zondervan.com. The "NIV" and "New International Version" are trademarks registered in the United States Patent and Trademark Office by Biblica, Inc.®

The names and details of the people and situations described in this book have been changed or presented in composite form in order to ensure the privacy of those with whom the authors have worked.

Cover design by Paula Gibson

Baker Publishing Group publications use paper produced from sustainable forestry practices and postconsumer waste whenever possible.

25 26 27 28 29 30 31   7 6 5 4 3 2 1

To my father, Roger Yarhouse,
who passed away during the writing
of this book and whose great love for the church
was passed down to his children.
—Mark Yarhouse

To Lauren, Johnny, and the friends I've met
through Revoice and Eden Invitation.
Without your witness and wisdom,
I wouldn't have been able to write this book.
—Julia Sadusky

CONTENTS

List of Sidebars   xi
Preface   xiii

PART 1   UNDERSTANDING CULTURE AND CONTEXT

1. A Culture of Sexual Identities   3
2. Queer Theory   39
3. How Sexual Identities Come into Being   67

PART 2   IDENTIFYING A MINISTRY MODEL

4. Controversies in Ministry   91
5. A Relational-Narrative Approach to Ministry   123
6. Narrative Revisited: Minister to Questions Tied to Chapters in a Life Story   147
7. Engaging Youth: Ministry Recommendations for Care and Counseling   165

Epilogue   197

Acknowledgments   199
Notes   201
Bibliography   215
Index   221

SIDEBARS

Key Terms and Emerging Sexual Identities   4

Microminoritized Identities   9

For Parents: Take a Long-Term View   24

For Parents: Set the Framework   28

For Parents: What Validation Is and Isn't   41

For Parents: Stay Engaged   68

For Parents: Stay Present and Invite Conversations   100

For Parents: Acknowledge and Be Curious About Terms   104

For Parents: Become a Cultural Ambassador   110

For Parents: Buffer Against Unhelpful Narratives   129

PREFACE

This book is an exploration of the rise in what we call "emerging sexual identities"—that is, newer labels for sexual attraction or sexual orientation that are sometimes used, especially by young people, in place of older words like "gay." These emerging sexual identities are often more precise expressions of sexual identity labels, whereas the dominant taxonomies (or categories) of gay, lesbian, and bisexual tend to be much broader. Of course, churches have already struggled to navigate the cultural shifts that led to the rise of gay, lesbian, and bisexual identities. Until emerging sexual identities are studied and understood, these newer labels may create an even wider chasm between the church and young people navigating sexual identity.

This book is primarily a resource for those working in formal ministry to youth and young adults, including parents and laypersons in Christian churches. We find that many Christians are concerned about the topic of sexual identity, love family members and friends who are exploring sexual identity or who have adopted an emerging sexual identity label (e.g., demisexual, omnisexual), and feel ill-equipped to navigate a landscape that continues to evolve rapidly. We intend this resource to be a reliable, measured call for thoughtful Christian engagement in a culture in which norms and dominant taxonomies for self-understanding and self-identity are changing. Further, we anticipate this book will assist you in more effectively accompanying youth today.

If you are picking up this book, you likely have many questions about emerging sexual identities: Where did these identities come from? How should we think about them? What should we do in response? What principles should guide our conversations around them? Although we, the authors, do not presume to have all the answers to questions like these, we hope to normalize the questions you do have, help you frame these questions in constructive ways, and provide a promising direction toward answers we are all seeking.

Part 1 of this book will guide you through our changing culture of sexual identities and consider how queer theory and other factors have shaped the context for emerging sexual identities. If you are hoping for clarity around the various factors contributing to the present landscape of sexual identity labels, this section will aim to offer a foundational framework. Part 2 will aim to assist you in parsing out your ministry model, whether you are a person in active ministry to youth or a layperson seeking to accompany your children, loved ones, colleagues, and friends. We will consider the various controversies related to several distinct ministry approaches. Then we will consider an approach to ministry that is rooted in forming deep relationships built on an understanding of the identity journeys of youth today. We will close this resource with a range of ministry recommendations that we hope will equip you to more effectively accompany the youth you care for.

The primary audience of this book is those in youth ministry. There are distinct questions related to ministry settings that we address in the text. At the same time, parents will also benefit from reading this book as they seek to accompany the youth they love. Parents will find practical suggestions for how to apply various principles in their role as parents, especially if their teen is exploring or adopting emerging sexual identities. Even if their teen is not a sexual minority, parents would do well to understand the sexual identity landscape today in order to effectively help their teen navigate it.

It is no easy feat to minister or to be a parent at any point in history, and the times we find ourselves in are no exception. Even as you likely bring concerns, questions, and hopes to this conversation, we want to encourage you to adopt a posture of curiosity as you dive into this resource. For parents, we hope you will see many applications to parenting your older children and teens as they are navigating questions around language and identity. Together, we will hope to gain clarity, conviction, compassion, and charity for the youth we are entrusted by God to accompany.

PART 1

UNDERSTANDING CULTURE AND CONTEXT

CHAPTER 1

A Culture of Sexual Identities

Helene, a seventeen-year-old high school senior, came in for her first therapy session on edge and hesitant to trust, as many people do. She had tried therapy one other time, but as she said, "The therapist didn't seem to know what to do with me." Her last therapist, a Christian therapist found by her parents, was visibly uncomfortable when Helene shared about her pattern of sexual attraction. I (Julia) took some time to normalize her concerns about opening up again to someone, especially after having an unhelpful therapy experience previously. We talked about how, since trust is earned and built over time, it may take time for her to be ready to share certain aspects of her story with anyone else, including me. I reiterated that I wanted to make space for Helene to share about her sexuality openly with me, and I knew that didn't happen for everyone right away. A few sessions later, Helene told me she wanted to talk more about her sexuality.

"I'm aromantic and asexual," Helene disclosed. "I used to think there was something wrong with me for not feeling attracted to anyone, so it helped to know there are other people like me. I finally feel like I belong somewhere."

I thanked Helene for having the courage to share about her experience with me. I asked how it felt to say those words. "Relieving," she said with a smile.

Even though I was familiar with the terms "aromantic" and "asexual," I asked her to elaborate on them a bit more: "What drew you to describe yourself as aromantic and asexual? What resonated for you when you first learned about those words?"

Helene shared how she had tried for a while to "force myself to like someone," until she read about "aromantic/ace" labels online two years ago. "It was good to have a word to explain to myself why I don't feel romantic or sexual desire for anyone," she said. "It clicked because, up until then, I just thought I was broken or something. Having a word meant that maybe I wasn't so messed up after all."

In this opening chapter, we introduce the origins of sexual identities, how our culture has embraced them, how they function for people, and what they mean to people like Helene today.

KEY TERMS AND EMERGING SEXUAL IDENTITIES

Below we define several terms you may encounter. We do this not to condone or commend each term but to provide a reference point for categories that young people in particular are readily drawing from today.

Ace spectrum: "Ace" stands for asexuality, a range of ways people identify as having an absence of sexual and/or romantic attraction.

Androsexual: "Sexual and romantic attraction to men, males, or masculinity . . . regardless of biology."*

Aroace: Refers to those who identify as both aromantic and asexual.

Aromantic: A person with minimal or no romantic feelings.

Aromantic spectrum: A range of ways in which people identify as having minimal or no romantic feelings.

Asexual: A person with minimal or no sexual attraction.

Biromantic: "Romantic attraction, but not sexual attraction, to people of more than one gender."†

Biromantic gay: Attraction to "various gender groups romantically but only sexually attracted to men." Other pairings with biromantic (which references romantic attraction) are biromantic lesbian, biromantic heterosexual, biromantic asexual, biromantic pansexual.‡

Bisexual: Sexual attraction to both sexes.

Bisexual polyamorous: A person attracted to both sexes and who has more than one partner.

Cupiosexual: "Asexual people who don't experience sexual attraction but still have the desire to engage in sexual behavior."†

Demiromantic: "People who experience romantic attraction only under specific circumstances, such as after building an emotional relationship with a person."†

Demisexual: "People who experience sexual attraction only under specific circumstances, such as after building a romantic or emotional relationship with a person."†

Gay: Sexual attraction to the same sex. It may also be used as an umbrella term for people who identify as lesbian, gay, and bisexual.

Grayromantic: People who identify as experiencing infrequent or less romantic attraction or romantic attraction under specific circumstances.

Graysexual: People who identify as experiencing infrequent or less sexual attraction or sexual attraction under specific circumstances.

Heteroflexible: Primary attraction to the opposite sex, while experiencing some romantic or sexual attraction to people of the same sex.**

Lesbian: A woman who is sexually attracted to the same sex.

Omnisexual: Similar to "pansexual," this refers to people whose "sexuality isn't limited to those of a particular gender, sex, or sexual orientation."†

Panromantic: The capacity for romantic feelings toward others regardless of sex, gender identity, or sexual orientation.

Pansexual: The capacity for sexual attraction toward others regardless of sex, gender identity, or sexual orientation.

Polysexual: "A sexual orientation that involves sexual or romantic attraction to people of varying genders" and an umbrella term for other labels such as "bisexuality, pansexuality, omnisexuality, and queer."†

Pomosexual: A person who does not use traditional or dominant sexual identity labels (e.g., gay, lesbian, bisexual, straight).

Private identity: The way a person identifies and labels their sexual attractions or orientation internally.

Public identity: The way a person seeks to be known by others through the use of labels in reference to their sexual attraction or orientation.

Queer: An umbrella term that can include "people who aren't exclusively heterosexual"† or who do not identify as cisgender.

Sexual attraction: The most descriptive way to express one's experience of sexual interest or draw to another person. A person might be sexually attracted to people of the same sex or opposite sex or both sexes.

Sexual identity: The labels people use to communicate about their sexual attractions or orientation.

Sexual orientation: When experiences of sexual attraction persist in direction and strength over the course of time.

Skoliosexual: Attraction to people who identify as "nonbinary, genderqueer or trans."†

Spectrasexual: Attraction to "multiple or varied sexes, genders, and gender identities, but not necessarily all or any."†

---

* Mere Abrams, "47 Terms That Describe Sexual Attraction, Behavior, and Orientation," Healthline, updated February 17, 2023, https://www.healthline.com/health/different-types-of-sexuality. This framing demonstrates how recent iterations of gender theory have shaped emerging sexual identities, where young people will separate sex and gender and not reference sex when expressing their attraction to someone. For Catholic readers, this departs from Catholic anthropology in meaningful ways. In Catholic anthropology, which is shared by many Protestants as well, "biological sex and the socio-cultural role of sex (gender) can be distinguished but not separated." "The Vocation and Mission of the Family in the Church and in the Contemporary World," Final Report of the Synod of Bishops to the Holy Father, Pope Francis, October 24, 2015, par. 58, https://www.vatican.va/roman_curia/synod/documents/rc_synod_doc_20151026_relazione-finale-xiv-assemblea_en.html, cited in Pope Francis, *Amoris Laetitia*, par. 56, https://www.vatican.va/content/dam/francesco/pdf/apost_exhortations/documents/papa-francesco_esortazione-ap_20160319_amoris-laetitia_en.pdf. This definition and others in this list also reflect how emerging gender identities have contributed to emerging sexual identity labels.

† Mere Abrams, "47 Terms That Describe Sexual Attraction, Behavior, and Orientation," Healthline, updated February 17, 2023, https://www.healthline.com/health/different-types-of-sexuality.

‡ Samuel Njoroge, "What Does It Mean to Be Biromantic?," LGBTQ and All, July 16, 2021, https://www.lgbtqandall.com/what-does-it-mean-to-be-biromantic.

** Sian Ferguson, "What Does It Mean to Be Heteroflexible?," Healthline, November 20, 2019, https://www.healthline.com/health/heteroflexible#What-does-it-mean.

Sexual Identity and Sexual Orientation

"Sexual identity," sometimes called "sexual orientation identity," refers to the labels people use to communicate their sexual attractions or orientation, both to others and to themselves. Sexual identity labels grew out of an identity-focused relationship between a person and their sexual orientation. By this we mean that people are now often asking, "How does the description of my sexual orientation inform my sense of self and personhood?" or, "How does my sexual orientation inform my understanding of my identity, of who I am?"

One facet within the development of sexual identity is the use and consideration of sexual identity labels (e.g., the self-defining attribution "I am gay"). Another facet is the cultivation of a sense of identity and culture in the act of adopting and embodying sexual identity labels. Sexual identity labels are adopted privately as one thinks about one's experience and connects that to existing taxonomies for sexual identity categorization. These labels are often also adopted publicly and in one's community to the extent that one adopts and expresses one's sexual identity label to others.

Given the expanding range of labels people are adopting both privately and publicly to communicate their sexual identity, we must begin by asking: How did sexual identities initially develop? Then we will consider how youth and young adults relate to the various categories historically offered and what terms have emerged as a result.

In terms of the initial development of sexual identities, the earliest sexual identities began as words developed for describing sexual orientation. Although sexual identity and sexual orientation are distinct concepts—"orientation" refers to patterns of attraction apart from the meaning assigned to those patterns, whereas "identity" refers to categories of self-understanding and public identification—the same labels are sometimes used for both. We have until quite recently thought of sexual orientations and identities as primarily including heterosexual (or "straight"), homosexual (including gay and lesbian), and bisexual (or "bi").

A subsequent question that arises is this: What changes have we witnessed in recent years in the degree to which certain terms are used by youth and young adults to talk about their sexual identity?

More recently, the words "homosexuality" and "homosexual" have largely fallen out of the vernacular, particularly among today's youth. The word "gay" has been retained as a much more common way to convey both orientation and sexual identity. At the same time, fewer young women are identifying as "lesbian" today, and they prefer "bi" or the use of "gay" as an umbrella term for their sexual orientation and identity.

When we refer to emerging sexual identities, we are referencing identity categories that have emerged in response to perceived inadequacies in the dominant models of sexual identity (i.e., gay, lesbian, bisexual). These emerging identities are largely curated by youth online in digital and social media, and they account for a microminoritized sense of identity—that is, people in a minority group developing even smaller and more granular minority identities.[1] For instance, The Trevor Project reported over one hundred sexual identity labels used by participants in their research.[2] Labels such as "demisexual," "skoliosexual," "spectrasexual," "graysexual," and "cupiosexual" (see the sidebar "Key Terms and Emerging Sexual Identities" for definitions).

These emerging sexual identities have expanded alongside emerging gender identities. We wrote about emerging gender identities previously.[3] These gender identities include "agenderflux," "androgyn," "trigender," "feminine-of-center," and "polygender." The mainstream cultural language has followed gender theory in expanding sexual identities to account for romantic, sexual, and emotional attraction to people who adopt different gender identities.

Microminoritized Identities

The phrase "microminoritized identities" refers to some young people's turn away from broader, more familiar categories (gay, transgender) to new terms that convey more specific experiences of gender or sexual identity (e.g., "I am androsexual" or "I am graygender"). These microminoritized identities are frequently combined across emerging sexual and gender identities (e.g., "I am a pansexual demiboy" or "I am a trigender graysexual").

We have seen an increased preference for these microminoritized identities in our research with college-aged sexual and gender minorities. For instance, in a recent study we conducted, we heard language such as "asexual heteroromantic," "demisexual heteroromantic," and "bisexual sapphic queer." Some participants explained their use (or lack of use) of sexual identity labels: "I am bisexual (but that is inclusive of more than two genders)" or "I try to come across as asexual at work, and try to code as straight when it benefits me." One participant shared, "I think I would not pick any label really, but use queer for conversations about sexuality."[4] This begs a third question: How is it that more dominant taxonomies have fallen out of favor and been replaced by these microminoritized identities?

MICROMINORITIZED IDENTITIES

Microminoritized identities are identity classifications that seek much greater specificity than the dominant taxonomy of gay, lesbian, bisexual, transgender, and nonbinary. In an effort to be precise, young people navigating sexual and gender identity often draw upon both emergent sexual *and* gender identity labels to convey their sense of self (e.g., bigender demiromantic), performing and cocurating these identities with their peers through digital and social media platforms.

Source: Cover, *Emergent Identities*, 43.

Three Typologies of Sexual Identity

Rob Cover, in his book *Emergent Identities*, argues that the micro-minoritized identities preferred by many young people are characteristic of *emergent* identities rather than *residual* or *dominant* identities. Cover draws this three-part typology from Raymond Williams, who uses the terms "residual," "dominant," and "emergent" to conceptualize how different social structures coexist and interact.[5] Cover suggests that this same language can help us understand sexual and gender identities as well. Let's explore how Cover applies each of Williams's three categories to sexual and gender identity language (see fig. 1.1).

Figure 1.1 Williams's three ways of conceptualizing social structures

Residual Taxonomy

As the word suggests, "residual" structures are residues, what remains of something that used to be a more substantial element. These are structures that were once dominant in a society but have since waned in prevalence. While they still offer shared categories for conceptualization and meaning, residual structures have fallen out of popularity and are slowly diminishing. Williams explains,

> The residual, by definition, has been effectively formed in the past, but it is still active in the cultural process. . . . Thus certain experiences, meanings, and values which cannot be expressed or substantially verified in terms of the dominant culture, are nevertheless

lived and practiced on the basis of the residue—cultural as well as social—of some previous social and cultural institution or formation.[6]

That which is residual still has sway in some circles of society, but it is waning in influence, as fewer people in a society share the same beliefs, practices, and formulations.

As it pertains to sexuality and gender, "residual" refers to previously dominant ways of conceptualizing sexual or gender identities that are now declining. There are remnants of these previously dominant categories still present in society, and they could be significant reference points in some segments of society, but they no longer have their former dominance. What had previously been dominant and is now residual in Western culture is reflected in the language and meaning or designation of certain terms.

One easy way to understand residual identities is to look at once-common language that is no longer preferred by the people it describes. (These ideas are addressed in more detail later in this chapter.) For example, the word "homosexual" was created in the nineteenth century to reflect a nonnormative sexual orientation. Likewise, the word "heterosexual" was created at the same time to reflect a normative sexual orientation.[7] Both words, especially "homosexual," reflected late Victorian medical and psychiatric understandings of nonnormative sexuality. Prior to this, sexuality was understood and thought of in reference to acts/behaviors, not identities. What was termed "homosexuality" was initially regarded as a vice and then as an abnormality. These framings were reflective of attempts to regulate sexuality.[8]

Most Christian churches have traditionally held sexual union between a man and a woman in the context of marriage to be in conformity with nature, whereas same-sex sexual acts, anal sex between a man and a woman, and certain other sexual acts are understood as contrary to nature. Christian teachings on sexual behavior, then, have historically recognized that certain opposite-sex sexual behaviors and all same-sex sexual behaviors are sinful, but there has been a recognition that opposite-sex sexual behavior is morally permissible in the context of a marriage between a man and a woman.[9]

The emphasis on moral regulation of sexuality that once belonged to religion was ultimately extended to psychiatry and institutions of mental health in the nineteenth and early twentieth centuries. This led to the shift from *vice* (as a religious category and meaning-making terminology) to *abnormality* (a psychiatric category and meaning-making terminology) for homosexuality in particular, whereas heterosexuality could be increasingly thought of as automatically virtuous and normative in society more broadly.[10] Once we shift from thinking of sexuality in terms of acts to identities, anything a man and a woman do together sexually is now cast as natural.

Obviously, these conceptualizations, tied to the words "homosexual" and "homosexuality," are growing faint in Western mainstream society. There are still elements of these conceptualizations in society; older psychiatric and medical frameworks may still reflect psychoanalytic conceptualizations of homosexuality. Additionally, various religions maintain the adherence to moral beliefs about sexual behavior that existed long before sexual orientations emerged as identity categories. However, the remaining residues of these terms and categories no longer carry as much weight in argument or significance in modern society as they once did.

Dominant Taxonomy

When it comes to cultural movements in sexual and gender identities, the shift from residual to dominant is a shift from "homosexuality" to terms like "gay," "lesbian," and "bisexual." It is also a shift from "lifestyle" to "immutable characteristics."

Dominant cultural and social processes are hegemonic, according to Williams.[11] They describe the way we currently engage a topic. In this discussion about sexuality, "dominant" refers to what are currently the most prominent conceptualizations of sexual identities. We most commonly refer today to lesbian, gay, and bisexual (LGB) people. These are the dominant categories for sexualities beyond heterosexual.

How did the shift from residual to dominant frameworks come about? Many cultural developments contributed to this shift, including elements of the sexual revolution in the 1970s. One significant path away from the residual structure toward the dominant one was biological (or genetic) essentialism. This dominant conceptualization suggests something innate and immutable; a person is "born this way," and their experience is unchanging. In the late twentieth and early twenty-first centuries, the dominant understanding leaned heavily on biological essentialism to argue for marriage equality and against sexual orientation change efforts (including both professional mental health conversion therapies and paraprofessional religious ministry interventions).

Tethering LGB interests to biology was risky. Ultimately, the cultural movement to connect LGB identity to biology helped facilitate the mainstreaming of LGB persons by framing orientation as an unchanging lifelong reality based on biological factors, such as prenatal hormonal exposure. Biological essentialism contributed to the mainstreaming of LGB identity in Western society. This conceptualization relied on liberal-humanist understandings for an "identity" argument of personhood. However, when orientation was presented as tied to biology in the way it has been, there was also the risk that these biological accounts of etiology (what causes people to be gay) could lead to some people attempting to intervene biologically and keep themselves from having gay kids. These preventative measures raised many bioethical questions. After all, attempts to understand the origins of same-sex sexuality and eliminate it were the main features of conversion therapies.

While conversion therapies did not usually rely on biological explanations for sexual orientation, they relied heavily on psychological explanations. Some conversion therapies, such as reparative therapy, highlighted people's childhood relationship with their same-gender parent or caregiver. If that relationship was characterized by emotional deprivation through abuse, neglect, or abandonment, reparative therapy theorized that those emotional deprivations could become sexualized in adolescence as a teenager went through puberty. Treatment, then, involved the formation of a nonsexual relationship with a same-gender adult, typically a therapist, who would offer an emotionally corrective relationship. The emotionally corrective relationship was said to facilitate a change in sexual orientation from homosexual to heterosexual.

Conversion therapies could have taken a similar approach but with an emphasis on biological essentialism. If specific markers from biology could be identified, would society move to prevent the development of a homosexual orientation? While scientists have not found a "gay gene" or anything comparable to it, many people in Western society today view being gay not as a choice but as something a person simply is—and this attitude was likely shaped by broad media coverage of research on biological factors (including prenatal hormonal exposure, genetic markers, and animal models) that contribute to same-sex orientation.[12]

Reliance on biological essentialism has been of interest to more than just the gay community; it has also felt beneficial to many within the straight community. As Cover observes, "The very idea of a gay gene helps to provide a 'discrete' identity for homosexuals, and thereby also for heterosexuals who without the particular gene cannot be at risk of slippage into homoerotic desires or behaviors."[13] As the gay community moved forward by following a civil rights model that had already been well established and successful, likening sexual orientation to race,[14] the straight community received a way of defining themselves as predictably and biologically different from gay people.

The idea that straight people and gay people are different on a biological level paved the way to expand social acceptance through an emphasis on equality. The argument in favor of legalizing same-sex marriage was rooted in such language, operating under the title of marriage "equality." This argument won the day in the United States when in 2015 the Supreme Court struck down state bans on same-sex marriage, legalizing such marriage across all states. Justice Anthony Kennedy, writing for the majority, reflects in the ruling:

> Until the mid-20th century, same-sex intimacy long had been condemned as immoral by the state itself in most Western nations, a belief often embodied in the criminal law. For this reason, among others, many persons did not deem homosexuals to have dignity in their own distinct identity. A truthful declaration by same-sex couples of what was in their hearts had to remain unspoken.[15]

This reflection on identity frames same-sex marriage as a right to the "dignity" to experience the fulfillment associated with marriage, as Kennedy goes on to write:

> No union is more profound than marriage, for it embodies the highest ideals of love, fidelity, devotion, sacrifice, and family. In forming a marital union, two people become something greater than once they were. As some of the petitioners in these cases demonstrate, marriage embodies a love that may endure even past death. It would misunderstand these men and women to say they disrespect the idea of marriage. Their plea is that they do respect it, respect it so deeply that they seek to find its fulfillment for themselves. Their hope is not to be condemned to live in loneliness, excluded from one of civilization's oldest institutions. They ask for equal dignity in the eyes of the law. The Constitution grants them that right.[16]

Advocacy for legal recognition of gay marriage is just the best-known outcome of a dominant taxonomy that emphasizes the biological components and likely permanence of sexuality; several other forms of societal acceptance are rooted in this same approach.

Although the dominant conceptualization of sexual orientation as innate and immutable has been compelling—particularly in research around twin studies, prenatal hormonal exposure, animal studies, and direct genetic markers of sexual orientation—it has also inspired research on the fluidity of sexuality, bridging the path from dominant to emergent conceptualizations. Lisa Diamond's research on sexual fluidity explored shifts not only in sexual identity but also in behavior, attractions, fantasies, and orientation. In some respects, Diamond's research suggested that some important elements of sexuality "changed without agency."[17] Put differently, Diamond was studying not whether sexual orientation changed as a result of therapy or ministry but rather whether sexual orientation, fantasy, attraction, and behavior ever changes naturally, or exhibits what she refers to as sexual "fluidity." Diamond followed seventy-nine sexual minority women over a decade and reported that they experienced changes, or fluidity, in their sexual identity and sexual behaviors more commonly than the prevailing view of stability implied.[18] In an interview about her results, Diamond says,

> What I found was that, as I tracked women's sexual attractions and sexual identities over time, regardless of where they started, whether they were lesbian, or bisexual, or some of the women were like, "well, I don't know what I am, but I'm somewhere," there was a lot of movement. As time went on, some of the women who started out as lesbian ended up falling in love with their male best friends and getting involved with them. Some of the women who were predominantly bisexual then ended up switching to be exclusively lesbian. And I just found that there was a lot more flexibility in women's sexuality than most of the literature at that time had suggested.[19]

Diamond's research challenged prevailing assumptions and served as a kind of bridge between what we now see as dominant and emergent formulations of sexual identity. Her more recent research has demonstrated greater fluidity in men as well as women than previously documented.[20] The most influential paradigm of sexuality is moving away from something innate and immutable toward something lived out and embodied. This new view is the hallmark of emergent sexualities, which we turn to next.

Emergent Taxonomy

The movement from dominant to emergent sexual identities is fascinating, entailing new insights into sexual attraction and orientation. It also demonstrates the concerns of a younger cohort and their exploration of what is possible, including the increasingly precise language they may use to process and express such possibilities.

Emergent expressions of sexual identities are both new and, in some ways, indebted to dominant sexual identities. Emergent conceptualizations are characterized by "new meanings and values, new practices, new relationships and kinds of relationships [that] are continually being created."[21] Indeed, by virtue of being emergent, they are new. At the same time, they are indebted to dominant sexual identities, since they are able to exist, in part, because the dominant sexual identities existed before them. There was sufficient opportunity, space, and permission to rework ways of thinking about oneself with reference to one's sexuality and gender. These emergent identities are "new articulations that arise not as processes isolated from the dominant but from new configurations of knowledge, meanings, values, practices and relationships."[22] To say that current taxonomies are emergent is to say that they are new and represent other possibilities than the dominant sexual identity taxonomy. The labels and categories for emergent sexual identities tend to be created largely by adolescents and young adults.

From an emergent understanding, the older taxonomies of heterosexual/homosexual (residual) and straight/LGB (dominant) reflect insufficient understandings of one's current experience. Young people appear to be looking for different and more specific frameworks: "There is clear evidence of very substantial interest among, particularly, younger people in working through the classificatory terms that comprise the new framework of diverse and proliferating gender and sexual identity labels."[23]

In a podcast on exploring sexuality, Aki Gormezano reflects on how some labels may be too narrow to account for the range of experiences today. This narrowness, Gormezano explains, is a criticism often made about the dominant taxonomy by those drawn to emergent taxonomies:

> I think when you just have identities and you just have labels, especially when identities and labels are really narrow . . . you might not have the language to articulate the ways in which you don't perfectly fit with that identity or label. And I think the more people who are able to understand the ways in which they might branch from their label or perfectly coincide with it, the more open everyone will be around, you know, just understanding that around each identity is a collection of people who might vary from that in different kinds of ways.[24]

Cover makes a similar observation about how emergent sexual identities may function for young people today:

> A proliferation of identity labels, norms, practices, desires, genders and subjectivities give, on the one hand, a new set of terms that might "catch" those who fell though the gaps of liveability and identity coherence previously and, on the other, a means of giving agency to young people, including the very vulnerable, to develop and articulate identity labels that might have a greater "fit" with

whatever disjuncture from normativity one might feel is going on in the practice of selfhood.[25]

Emergent Identities and the Dominant Taxonomy

According to Cover, emergent sexual and gender identities rely to some extent on dominant taxonomies as a launching point for the production of "new configurations, meanings, values and practices." The emergent is not completely divorced from the dominant in this regard: "The new emergent framework for gender and sexuality includes more than simply the flourishing of individual labels, categories and classifications."[26] The dominant serves as a starting point for new and novel exploration of sexual identity.

The emergent depends upon the dominant, but it is also different from the dominant in several ways, including a move away from the biological essentialism that was so important in the 1990s and early 2000s. The emergent framework shifts from conceptualizing sexuality as "innate, given and 'born that way'" toward a focus on how sexuality is "thought, enacted, embodied, represented and practiced."[27] The conceptualizations of the dominant framework were important historical precursors for emergent sexual identities, but emergent conceptualizations are divergent in meaningful ways (see table 1.1).

The emergent taxonomy is also different from the dominant in its shift away from "undoing of norms" toward "a call for belonging and awareness."[28] To the extent that the dominant paradigm is being challenged by the emergent, there is a sense in which the dominant had established its own norms that are currently being challenged.[29]

To say that emergent identities launch from dominant understandings is to say that they are still indebted to a sense of personhood found in the dominant taxonomy. They are not so much at odds with dominant identities as they are reflecting layers of

Table 1.1
Residual, Dominant, and Emergent Typologies

	Residual	Dominant	Emergent
Identity	Homosexual	Gay, lesbian, bisexual	Graysexual, pomosexual, semisexual, demisexual, etc.
Etiology	Lifestyle (moral) or late Victorian medical and psychiatric conceptualizations; nonnormative sexuality	Innate, immutable, "born that way"; biological essentialism	Enacted, practiced, embodied
Purpose	Regulating sexual behavior	Tolerance and equality	New meanings, practices, and identities
Framing	Vice, abnormality, psychopathology, mental illness	Assimilation, rights, culture to be recognized legally, culture to be celebrated	Cocuration of social identities by younger people to reflect alternatives to dominant taxonomy

Adapted from Cover, *Emergent Identities*, 99–127.

potential complexity that the dominant can only suggest: "What might be said to be happening here is a proliferation of identity labels and practices that help accommodate complexity, intersectionality and fluidity into an existing liberal-humanist understanding of identity, subjectivity and selfhood."[30] This new taxonomy is notably different from previous understandings that relied upon or leveraged various institutional authorities in making their claims.

The residual taxonomy relied on religious understandings of vice and psychiatric perceptions of pathology to create homosexual and heterosexual identities. The dominant taxonomy relied on experts in biology and social sciences to determine what counted as knowledge about innate and immutable sexual orientation identities. In contrast to both of these approaches, emergent taxonomies exist and are curated independent of expert opinion.

Let's return to the precision or granularity found in emergent sexual identities. As we indicated earlier in the chapter, microminoritized sexual and gender identities reflect ways young people utilize more specific language to identify themselves, often accounting for elements of *both* sexual and gender identity. For example, a young person might identify as an aromantic demigirl, a trigender aromantic, a pangender sapiosexual, or a nonbinary graysexual. They may or may not be attracted to the same sex. The ace spectrum describes people who do not experience attraction toward others; yet they often identify as part of the LGBTQ+ community (as we discuss further below). The inclusion of asexual people and others who don't experience attraction to the same sex within the LGBTQ+ umbrella is another key difference between dominant and emergent sexual and gender identity labels; the formerly clear distinction between gay and straight breaks down along the ace spectrum. Similarly, the clear distinction between gay and trans as two different kinds of communities blurs together under the emerging paradigm. Whereas "gay" and "lesbian" sexual identity labels focus only on sexuality, and the "transgender" label focuses only on gender identity, emerging identities are more likely to merge sexual and gender conversations within a single self-identification. This shift likely reflects the rising percentage of trans and nonbinary youth and young adults who identify their sexuality using more specific identity designations, which we will discuss below.

As we noted earlier, as gender terms and identities have expanded, so have sexual orientation and identity categories. The dominant taxonomy, which precedes the emergent expansion of gender terms, has men, women, or both together as the reference point for the direction of romantic or sexual attraction (e.g., "gay," "lesbian," "bisexual"). Because the mainstream Western philosophical framework of gender has shifted and asserted that gender was not tied to a person's biological sex, the labels and identities to discuss attraction also emerged without reference to a person's biological sex. This presents challenges for ministry since Christian anthropology has anchored sexual identity in embodiment and has historically understood the norms of sex and gender to be centered on biological sex. Recent shifts in cultural norms of sex and gender have and will have an impact on identity formation, both broadly and specifically as it relates to sexual orientation.

Youth Relationship to Emergent Taxonomies

Regardless of the origins of these terms, microminoritized identities carry emotionality and depth for many young people, which is why ministry approaches will fall flat if they dismiss these categories as merely excessive or unnecessary. Though we may have concerns about the way gender theory has shaped the current landscape, we want to recognize why youth find these terms compelling. A teen's unique configuration of identities is *theirs*: "It is clear that 'depth of feeling' is one very important aspect of how we can read the *meaningfulness of* these terms, the *attachment to* the new labels and *regard for* the taxonomy of labels itself."[31]

There are also many options for attraction beyond what people think of as sexual or romantic. These include, for example, platonic attraction (a desire for closeness in a relationship that is typically not sexual or romantic), aesthetic attraction (appreciation for the beauty in another), and sensual attraction (in which a person wishes for tactile interactions with another, such as cuddling or hugging).[32]

Younger people who adopt emergent sexual identities also seem to reflect different experiences with those identities. In a podcast interview about the process of "trying on" sexual identity labels to discern the comfort and fit of those labels, Stacy Watnick shared:

> We kind of try labels on like clothes. . . . I'm gonna try this sort of sweater on and see: Does that feel snuggly? Do I feel comfortable? Is there a resonance in my body and in my mind and my heart and my genitals, all over me, that this feels true . . . ? And much like the

sweater I put on, I don't have to wear it all the time. . . . There's a very flexible return policy on this kind of content: if they decide they don't want it, they don't have to keep it. But we're trying it on. Let's see how it feels.[33]

Compared to the finality with which residual labels (like "homosexual") and dominant labels (like "gay," "lesbian," and "bisexual") have been adopted, this reversible process of "trying on" sounds like a more casual way of exploring sexual and gender identity labels. We have known young people who do this: try on different labels, exchange one label for another, and even revisit previously significant labels. Some do not seem especially anxious about this process, seeming to treat it in the carefree way Watnick describes. However, other young people have expressed valid concern that this exploration and "trying on" of sexual and gender identity labels is not quite as carefree as they have been told.

For example, Cover raises a concern about younger people trying on microminoritized identity labels, especially when they do so through digital and social media.[34] He observes that these performances of identity often occur in communities attuned to policing for personal authenticity: Are you who you say you are? His concern is that as identity is tried on and practiced, embodied and rehearsed, it can also be scrutinized and policed for authenticity in ways young people may not be prepared for. They may experience their peers' scrutiny as an added stressor in identity exploration. To return to the clothing analogy introduced above: The way young people try on emerging sexual identities in front of one another is like trying on clothes in front of people who are critiquing those clothes' fit on you and sharing their opinions with all your friends through social media.[35] If the label or clothing you choose fits well and earns the approval of others, this could be an incredibly reinforcing and solidifying experience. If your peers disagree with the clothes' fit or authenticity on you, their criticism could contribute to deepened uncertainty and anxiety about your identity expression. You might experience some undue pressure to embody and perform your chosen clothes in ways that are distressing to you. You might not feel the freedom to try on other options.[36] The casualness in Watnick's account of testing labels reflects the current assumptions surrounding the creation of one's identity. While the idea of trying on and testing labels has been the experience of some young people we know, it has not been every young person's experience.

FOR PARENTS: TAKE A LONG-TERM VIEW

You may be wondering what to do if your young person is exploring emerging sexual identities. If they adopt a certain label, does that determine the course of their life? Should you attempt to dissuade them from this? Should you assume it's a phase they will eventually move through? We recommend neither that you assume such labels determine their entire life trajectory nor that you think of it as a phase. When a parent reacts out of fear of future outcomes and attempts to focus exclusively on controlling a teen's use of labels, teens often dig in their heels and continue to identify as such, just secretly. They will simply stop bringing parents into these conversations. Conversely, when a parent assumes that this is a phase and fails to interact at all with their teen's journey, the teen is left to navigate such questions alone or solely with the support of peers and media. We unpack helpful approaches throughout this book, but for now we want to remind you that efforts to either control your teen's use of language or refrain from understanding it further will leave teens left without you as a sounding board at a time when they still need you as a resource. Occupying this space can be difficult, because it is precisely when teens are signaling they have no need of their parents that they need their parents. Your teen will benefit immensely as you (1) calmly invite their questions and exploration, (2) express belief in their ability to navigate these waters with you and others by their side, (3) encourage their ability to critically think about information they are receiving from multiple sources, including media and peers, and (4) genuinely offer your own questions as they share their journey with you.

The Ace Spectrum

We suggested earlier that today's LGBTQ+ community seeks solidarity across a wide variety of experiences and identity labels, including among those who are not attracted to the same sex but want to convey affiliation with or adjacency to the LGBTQ+ community. These individuals may align with LGB and transgender people in their desire to exist outside of established norms for sexuality and gender. Most notably, this group includes those who identify with asexuality and the ace spectrum.

Asexuality has been defined by the Asexual Visibility and Education Network (AVEN) as "not experiencing sexual attraction or an intrinsic desire to have sexual relationships." Asexual people (aces) are described as existing on a spectrum called the ace spectrum. In the view of AVEN, asexuality is best conceptualized as an orientation rather than being viewed as simply low sex desire within another orientation or as some kind of pathology (such as a hyposexual desire disorder).

According to one estimate, about 1 percent of the population identifies as asexual.[37] Accurate estimation has been difficult, though, because larger representative studies have historically not had asexuality as an option for respondents' sexual orientation. The unreliability of self-report and disagreements about how to define asexuality also create challenges in gathering accurate data. Despite these challenges, many organizations currently use this 1 percent statistic. Surveys of the LGBTQ+ community have indicated that 1.7 percent of adults[38] in the LGBTQ+ community identify as asexual, and those estimates increase dramatically (to as high as 10 percent of the LGBTQ+ youth)[39] when youth are surveyed.

A surprisingly large percentage (41 percent) of asexual youth also identify as transgender or nonbinary, according to data from The Trevor Project.[40] Another 13 percent of asexual youth in the same survey were questioning whether they were trans or nonbinary. As is often the case with emerging microminoritized social identities, young people's LGBTQ+ identities frequently include both emerging sexual and gender designations, as when a young person identifies "aromantic demigirl" or "nonbinary graysexual." Those who identify along the ace spectrum may identify with the LGBTQ+ community either by virtue of their asexuality or by virtue of their gender identity or both.

More females than males identify as asexual. The Ace Community Survey Team reported that 55 percent of those surveyed identified as women/female, while 15 percent identified as men/male, 27 percent as nonbinary, and the remainder as other gender designations.[41]

AVEN defines several experiences along the ace spectrum, including demisexual ("someone who can only experience sexual attraction or desire after an emotional bond is formed") and graysexual ("someone who identifies with the area between asexuality and sexuality"). They also discuss variations in romantic and aromantic interests, including panromantic, biromantic, and aromantic.[42]

Susan McQuillan adds several more identities along the ace spectrum: quoisexual or quoiromantic (someone "confused or unsure about the difference between a platonic and sexual or romantic relationship"), cupioromantic or cupiosexual (someone "who wants a romantic or sexual relationship but doesn't experience romantic or sexual attraction"), and apothisexual (someone who is "not only asexual but also is repulsed by the idea of a sexual experience").[43]

In a dialogue on experiences within the ace spectrum, people introduced themselves in a variety of ways: "Gray Ace Cis-Woman," "aromantic, asexual, and a demigirl," "Cisgender woman, alloromantic asexual," "biromantic, sex-averse, asexual cisgendered woman," "queer and asexual cisgender woman," "cis-gendered female who is heteroromantic asexual," and "aro-ace woman."[44]

McQuillan asks the question, "Why all these labels?" Her thought is that "language has had to grow to include specific terms for new ideas to form and be understood and for self-identities to be recognized, and to allow for clear communication so that people can learn more from each other about different human experiences and perspectives. Sexual and gender labels help with all of these processes."[45]

This may be true, to some extent. There do appear to be some meaningful differences in the wide range of people who identify as being on the ace spectrum. For example, Daniel Copulsky and Phillip Hammack report on a survey of people who identify as on the ace spectrum, specifically asexual, graysexual, and demisexual individuals. Those who identify as asexual were "the least likely [compared to those who identified as graysexual or demisexual] to be in a relationship, experience romantic attraction, or identify with orientation labels signifying genders of attraction such as straight, bisexual, heteroromantic, and biromantic." While sexual interest and romantic interest could be named separately, asexual persons tended to identify as aromantic, while graysexual persons were "the most likely to identify as grayromantic, and demisexual individuals the most likely to identify as demiromantic." Perhaps not surprisingly, "asexual individuals also scored the lowest on measures of sex drive, personal disposition toward engaging in sex, and masturbation frequency."[46]

In a study of asexual individuals who were either romantic or aromantic, Ana Carvalho and David Rodrigues found that "aromantic asexual individuals identified more with asexuality," had "a more avoidant attachment style," and were "more concerned with relationship commitment." In contrast, romantic asexual individuals had "less sex aversion, more sexual experiences (both past and current), and more sexual partners in the past."[47]

How do Christians engage the ace spectrum? How should we think about it? We want to fold our answer into how we think about emerging sexual identities in general. We do not find it helpful to reduce our engagement to a kneejerk reaction to these identities. Nor do we suggest that Christians ought to believe these sociocultural shifts in language and social identities are always helpful, constructive, and consistent with Christian anthropology.

Rather, we want to start by gaining a better understanding of how emerging sexual and gender identities, including those along the ace spectrum, function for people. Why are young people drawn to these labels? How do they capture something that previous labels did not capture? How do they function for young people in relation to their peers, both in real life and on digital and social media platforms? These questions matter to us both as clinicians and as people engaged in Christian ministry, and these questions matter to parents as well.

Ministry is best offered out of genuine curiosity and interest in the person who finds emerging identities to be meaningful expressions of their experience or personhood. Once we've listened curiously, we may have important wisdom or challenges to offer those who use these labels; we can help them evaluate how their words function and how that function fits within growth

FOR PARENTS: SET THE FRAMEWORK

Parents are often the last ones to know about a young person's exploration of emerging sexual identities. Which means parents might also be the last to speak into this as well. We recommend that parents begin by talking with youth about attractions more broadly between the ages of ten and twelve. This allows parents to set the framework that attractions will begin to happen and invite youth to share future questions they may have about attractions or lack thereof. It will also help to remind teens that they will hear others speak about attractions and wonder about crushes, dating, and so on. Remind your teen, "There's nowhere else we'd rather you go with these questions than to us as your parents." This approach signals to teens that you are equipped to receive those questions but will not overexpose your teen if that language and those categories are not on their mind.

in Christlikeness. But we advise starting these conversations in a nonadversarial way, so that insofar as we are invited to speak into the lives of others, we understand more deeply the people we are speaking with.

A Brief History of Heterosexuality

It may be helpful to take a look at the history of heterosexuality as a construct. We do this to remind the reader that categories based on identity, like heterosexual or heterosexuality, are just that—categories. We are so familiar with these terms now that we may be under the impression that they always existed.

It's important to note that sex distinctions themselves are not socially constructed. The reality that male and female bodies are uniquely designed to form a complete procreative unity is not constructed. Considering sexuality in terms of identity instead of sexual acts or behavior emerged very recently in history. In this way, terms such as "heterosexual" and "heterosexuality" *are* socially constructed. They are linguistic terms used to account for what would be deemed as normative sexuality and gave way to thinking of sexuality in terms of identity as well. In our not-so-distant past (before 1869), people did not think of themselves or refer to themselves as heterosexual. They did consider sexuality in reference to behavior, and many would have norms and moral frameworks for sexual expression. The language of "heterosexual," though, did not yet exist. As historian Hanne Blank puts it,

> Prior to that time, men and women got married, had sex, had children, formed families, and sometimes even fell in love, but they were categorically not heterosexuals. They didn't identify themselves as "being" something called "heterosexual." They didn't think of themselves as having a "straight" sexual identity, or indeed have any awareness that something called a "sexual identity" even

existed. They couldn't have. Neither the terms nor the ideas that they express existed yet.[48]

"Heterosexual" was not a category or term that existed until the late nineteenth century. Despite behavior that reflected heterosexuality, the language was not yet available for self-reference: "Sexual behaviors, of course, were identified and catalogued, and often times, forbidden. But the emphasis was always on the act, not the agent."[49]

Blank goes on to say,

> No matter how formal the name sounds, heterosexuality was not, after all, developed as a scientific concept or according to anything like scientific principles.... The idea of something called the "heterosexual" was developed by non-scientists, specifically for use in the non-scientific milieu of the law. From its very inception, "heterosexual" was about people in social entities, participating in social and sexual interactions with one another, in the larger context of their society and their nations and national legal codes.[50]

It is also important to recognize that the development of the term "heterosexual" occurred during a shift in authority from religion to science, medicine, and psychiatry. It accounted for common practices and provided language for a norm that was evident to those who were concerned about threats to the family in society.[51]

The first record of the word "heterosexual" is in a letter written May 6, 1868, by Karl Maria Kertbeny. Kertbeny was a Hungarian journalist who used four terms to describe various sexual experiences: "heterosexual," "homosexual," "monosexual" (masturbation), and "heterogenit" (bestiality).[52] The word "heterosexual" would be used eventually to account for—and to some degree, regulate—sexual behavior beyond a religious paradigm. The rising popularity of the word represented a move away from religious designations of sexuality through the lenses of sin, vice, and degeneracy.

The backstory to Kertbeny's work is that new civil codes were being written to account for a wide range of sexual behaviors deemed "unnatural." These civil codes drew upon a mixture of science, observation of nature, and religion. Among the sexual behaviors deemed unnatural was sex between two men.[53] Kertbeny and a lawyer and journalist named Karl Ulrichs opposed including sex between two men in this civil code. Their opposition to this penal code was the context in which the word and concept of "heterosexual" was introduced. For Kertbeny, the parallel language of "homosexual" and "heterosexual" promoted the equality of two kinds of men with different sexual attractions, both of whom were equally recognized through this new taxonomy.[54]

Heterosexuality was not yet widely understood as it is today: as a sexual orientation, an opposite-sex sexuality. Rather, heterosexuality would be defined in different ways over the next few decades. In fact, rather than describing typical levels of opposite-sex attraction, "heterosexual" was sometimes used to portray out-of-control or aberrant desires for opposite-sex sex. For example, James Kiernan referred to heterosexuality in a medical journal in 1892 as a "psychiatric hermaphroditism" characterized by "abnormal methods of gratification" ("abnormal" here meaning nonprocreative).[55] The early twentieth century would see heterosexuality as "associated with human 'need,' 'drive,' or 'instinct' for propagation."[56] It would take time for doctors (and then for the wider public) to think of heterosexuality as we do today, as an orientation to the opposite sex and a norm that contrasts with other orientations and patterns of attraction.

Of note, "heterosexual" and "heterosexuality" remain part of the dominant taxonomy today, although the corresponding terms "homosexual" and "homosexuality" have fallen out of dominance and are considered residual. Whereas "homosexual" and "homosexuality" carry negative connotations of religious vice or psychiatric classification in many people's minds, "heterosexual" and "heterosexuality" are currently understood by most speakers as fairly neutral.

What does the future hold for heterosexuality as a construct?[57] Many queer theorists argue that because there was a time before the concept of heterosexuality existed, there could be a time when it falls out of our vernacular as well. It could follow the path of "homosexual" and become residual. While this is possible, we see it as unlikely to become residual in the immediate future, as it remains a widely used self-referent for a considerable percentage of people.

Before we close this chapter, we want to discuss other nonnormative sexualities and behaviors. We do this because we are often asked about whether they should be included in the conversation about emerging sexual identities.

Other Nonnormative Sexualities and Behaviors

Kyle came into a session with me (Julia) visibly troubled. He had sent an email before the session, saying, "There's something I need to talk about that I feel some confusion about. It's kind of taboo, so I'm not quite sure how to begin."

After he sat down and took some time to get settled, he started to share: "I've been trying out consensual nonmonogamy for the past few months, and I can't seem to figure out if it's right for me. I said yes to it initially, but if I'm honest, I had no clue what it would actually feel like to know my partner was in a relationship with someone else. I thought it would still work, because I hate the pressure I often feel in relationships to show up for someone perfectly all the time. I thought this could be a solution for me, where I didn't have to be everything to someone. As time went on, I feel like I've felt in other relationships—that I'm not enough. At the same time, I've heard it can be really good for people. Maybe I need to adjust to it, and then I'll feel better."

Kyle's story captures another emerging clinical and ministry concern. We are asked at times whether nonnormative sexual behaviors not named by the LGBTQ+ acronym are also part of emerging sexual identities. These can include experiences such as consensual nonmonogamy (CNM); bondage and discipline, domination and submission, sadism, and masochism (BDSM); and kink. Should we think of these behaviors as emerging sexual identities in the same way we think of the ace spectrum, pansexuality, omnisexuality, pomosexuality, and other terms? Is Kyle coming into a new identity as he explores CNM?

Generally speaking, we do not see nonnormative sexual behaviors like CNM, BDSM, and kink as part of emerging sexual identities. People who engage in behaviors such as BDSM and kink include both straight people and members of the LGBTQ+ community. Also, a portion of both gay and straight people enter into consensually nonmonogamous relationships. There may be a greater tolerance for CNM, BDSM, and kink within the mainstream LGBTQ+ community simply because these communities share a nonnormative designation and social stigma, but we find this to be less true within Christian LGBTQ+ circles. Further, we are aware that many teens are concerned about the emergence of these behaviors, while others see them as problematic but are still being shaped by them online and through peers.[58]

Some people who practice BDSM view it as behavior independent from sexual identity, while others view their BDSM/kink as sexual orientation and identity. Margaret Nichols and James Fedor compare the identity development process of someone in BDSM to early-stage models of identity development among gay males and lesbians.[59] Similarly, some people see kink as behavioral ("doing kink"), while others view it as identity ("being kinky").[60] In either case, a person's sexual orientation or pattern of attraction toward one or more genders does not determine interest in role play, fantasy, BDSM, and so on. Straight and gay people alike may participate in such activities in their sexual life.

Along these lines, for some in the BDSM/kink community, the desire to characterize their experience as sexual orientation may be motivated by a desire to follow the success of the LGBTQ+ community in finding mainstream social acceptance.[61] Arguments about the innate or immutable nature of such interests, based on biological essentialism, could be a part of that discussion. Likewise, efforts to increase mainstream portrayals of the BDSM/kink community are also reminiscent of some LGBTQ+ activist efforts. The *Fifty Shades of Grey* books and movies (however misleading they may be) are one prominent example of the mainstreaming of BDSM/kink. In our clinical practices, we have witnessed many young people exposed to this content through social media as well, which introduces concerning pornographic content, themes, and sexual behaviors that are harmful to youth mental health and identity development.[62]

In general, however, we would not equate the mainstreaming of nonnormative practices such as BDSM, kink, and CNM with the developing expansiveness of the emerging and microminoritized sexual and gender identities we describe in this book. While we are called as Christians to critically evaluate both sets of experiences and recognize points of concern for Christians, we can do this best when we recognize their important differences from one another. Doing so protects us from making a caricature of sexual and gender identities, as if they were simply another iteration of the efforts to normalize sexual behaviors tied to BDSM, kink, and CNM.

Concluding Thoughts

As we bring this chapter to a close, we want to return to the distinction between residual, dominant, and emergent taxonomies as they apply to emerging sexual identities. Your primary frame of reference may be closest to the residual framework: You may understand same-sex sexual behaviors as reflective of a mental health concern (even if mainstream contemporary mental health associations no longer view them that way). It's common for conservative Christians (and Jews and Muslims, among others) to be more familiar with residual language like "homosexual" because such terms seem to lend themselves to upholding a moral framework in which same-sex sexual behaviors are deemed morally impermissible. Without further exploration, we might not realize that the historical shift to such terms can be used to normalize all heterosexual acts as permissible, even those at odds with a Christian understanding of sexual ethics. This leads to many churches using language that is far removed from the language and categories of the broader culture today and can unintentionally imply in our communities that heterosexual sexual behavior is always virtuous and allowable, whatever form it takes. That gap between church and culture, between religious faith and emerging sexual identities, will only grow over time in this context. We recommend that you use precise language whenever possible. For example, if a church is offering teaching on sexual ethics, rather than using terms like "heterosexuality" and "homosexuality," it could do so using a framework for sexual behavior that clearly identifies what is morally permissible and applies to all church attendees. Describing morality in terms of behaviors, not identities, may help us move away from language that is at least partially residual (e.g., "homosexuality") and less accessible to youth.

We want to close this chapter by reminding you that the question "Am I normal?" is often a driving question for adolescents and emerging adults. Remember the story of Helene that started this chapter. She, like many youth who are exploring identity, is relieved by labels that communicate "belonging and normalcy" in a time of life when it *is* normative to seek out identity and belonging. As one author puts it, "The question *Am I normal?* continues to play a very substantial role in young people's lives."[63]

We have seen in this first chapter that what is understood as normal has expanded in our society. Cover makes this observation about asexuality (and nonbinary identity), but it could equally be applied to all emerging sexual identities:

> Perhaps the most important thing here is that what counts as normal has grown, such that a gender identity which is nonbinary or a sexuality which classifies itself as asexual enter the range of possibility of being considered normal and normal categories with which one can identify with coherence, intelligibility and recognition.[64]

At one point in time, Christianity could count on some convergence between religious values and conceptualizations in the fields of psychology and psychiatry. Despite a historical shift in authority, the remnants of Christian normative structures were deeply impactful in some of the earliest scientific, psychiatric, and medical designations of normal and healthy sexuality and sexual desire. These designations are no longer dominant. Our society has moved to a new dominant taxonomy of sexualities, and young people are developing an emergent taxonomy.

While "what is normal" has expanded in culture, "what is normal" has not expanded in the same way (or with reference to the same categories of sexuality and sexual identity) in Christian churches. What is normal in middle school and high school, for example, is much more expansive than what is normal in Sunday school and youth group. Many churches are uncomfortable not only with emerging sexual identities but also with dominant categories for sexual identity. As that distance between these competing visions of "normal" grows—and we predict that it will continue to grow—we must ask how Christians are called to respond.

You are ministering or parenting in a cultural moment in which dominant and emergent conceptualizations are most salient. The challenge we will turn to in the second half of this book is how ministers can position themselves to minister effectively when the surrounding culture sees their primary orienting framework and meaning-making structures as residual. This is not an entirely new phenomenon, but it presents unique challenges in ministry spaces in every age.

Now that we have mapped the shifting taxonomies we see today, we want to zoom out to the larger context for these shifts. After all, you are likely wondering, "How have emergent conceptualizations become so readily adopted?" To say they are preferred by youth doesn't tell us how that has occurred. One major contributor, the salience of queer theory, is what we now turn to.

CHAPTER 2

Queer Theory

Danny, a sophomore in college who currently identifies as pansexual and previously wondered if he was nonbinary as well, came into his session feeling angry and confused. Danny had been attending a Christian Bible study for the past month at the invitation of an older sibling. "I love learning about the Bible and am so curious to see what other people think of it," he said. "But I don't think I can go back."

"What happened?" I (Julia) asked.

"This week, things got political," he recalled. "We went from reading in the book of Hebrews to someone going on a tangent about how disgusted they are with the 'delusional people' who believe 'this queer theory crap.' It happened out of nowhere, and I felt like if they knew about me being drawn to queer theory, they would kick me out of the group or embarrass me in front of everyone. I tried to speak up and say, 'I don't think everyone who agrees with that is delusional.' The person who made the original comment rolled their eyes and said, 'You can't really believe that!'"

Danny went on: "No one else said anything. That was the most disappointing part. It's fine if you don't agree with a theory, but you don't have to be so judgmental about the people who might be fans of it. I don't even know that I agree with everything in queer theory, but I don't think I'm delusional for being curious about it."

I asked Danny how he felt about returning to the group. "I just don't know that it's the place for me," he said. "I like being challenged, but I have a hard time being around people who talk that way about people I know and care about."

Danny did go back to the group, but only after some encouragement to engage with peers, even those with different perspectives, and to give feedback to his friends in those conversations when he felt as if they were being unkind in their comments.

Danny's experience and hesitancy to return to these environments isn't unique. How we talk about queer theory, engage critically with it, and respond to people drawn to it has everything to do with how we evangelize in the modern era.

Why Queer Theory?

How can it be that queer theory, and a Christian's engagement with it, could be salient enough to lead a person to question being part of a Christian community? This speaks to the power of queer theory in shaping the frameworks of many of our youth, whether or not they are aware of its impact. While we don't suggest that you consider your primary ministry and parenting approach being one of cognitive engagement in queer theory, having some frame of reference for its role in the shaping of emerging sexual identities will help you situate some of the ideas we will discuss within a broader framework.

The need to discuss queer theory in a book by psychologists on sexual identity labels may not be obvious at first. Certainly, there are other Christians whom we recommend you turn to for a more robust treatment of queer theory.[1] Yet we have learned to engage queer theory as Christian psychologists for a range of reasons.

In some ways, encountering queer theory is inescapable when one works in LGBTQ+ research and the mental health field more broadly. Many of the prominent voices in psychology are impacted by queer theory and subscribe to it. This means that, as Christian psychologists, we have been invited to engage with this theory, even as we have questions about its philosophical assumptions.

FOR PARENTS: WHAT VALIDATION IS AND ISN'T

In reading about Danny's experience here, how would you handle this situation as a parent of a college student? You might consider validating Danny's hesitancy to step back into this environment. Many parents worry that validation signals agreement with everything their child is thinking and feeling or that validation requires you to pretend you have the same reference points. But actually validation simply says, "I see you and I hear you where you are, and it makes sense that you feel that way."

On the other hand, your reaction might be to say it makes perfect sense that Danny wouldn't want to go back. Most of us prefer environments where people agree with us. It can be difficult, especially in polarized climates, to step into a space where people cannot see the appeal of queer theory. After validating his hesitancies, you may also want to reflect the value of him developing assertiveness in environments where people disagree. People tend to dismiss what they don't understand, and it might be helpful to let Danny see that there can be value in being in relationship with people where he asks for respect in spite of disagreements.

If you have concerns about queer theory, you could genuinely share that: "I, too, have struggled with aspects of queer theory and at times have had difficulty speaking charitably. But despite our differences, I am grateful for these conversations that help us come to a deeper understanding together." You might ask Danny, "What are they not understanding about queer theory and your draw to it?" Another helpful approach could be something like this: "With any theory, there are usually things that you don't fully resonate with. Are there pieces of queer theory you wrestle with?" This can build Danny's own critical thinking and ability to see through the eyes of those who might also wrestle with it.

We have also witnessed queer theory's influence moving beyond the academic circles we operate in. Some theories remain within the ivory tower of academia, whereas others seep into the very fabric of society. Through our own engagement of queer theory, we see the latter.

For the purpose of this book, we recognize that queer theory is profoundly invested in challenging and deconstructing norms in our society more broadly. The norms challenged include not only notions of heterosexuality as normative but also those around the terms "gay," "lesbian," and "bisexual"—the dominant taxonomies within the LGBTQ+ community and broader culture. Queer theory challenges the dominant taxonomies and attempts to move beyond them. In some ways, queer theory informs steps taken to identify and validate emerging sexual identities and microminoritized identities. Further, we are seeing some Christians begin to engage with queer theory, with some actively opposing it and an increasing number seeking to integrate aspects of it into Christian thought around sexuality. In light of this, in this chapter we look at the development of queer theory and consider Christian responses and engagement in light of our discussion of emerging sexual identities.

Defining Queer Theory

With this in mind, we want to offer our own reflections on queer theory. We will begin with defining the term. In 1991, Teresa de Lauretis used the term "queer theory" in the introduction of a special issue of the journal *differences*. Although queer theory has many roots (e.g., feminism, the gay movement, AIDS activism,[2] and so on), it is most associated in academic settings with gender and sexuality studies and related concepts from both gay and lesbian studies and feminist studies.

Queer theory is intellectually indebted to the French philosopher Michel Foucault, who viewed sexuality as socially constructed (shaped and made real by social conventions, processes, and practices within a society). In addition to Foucault, influential queer theorists include Gayle Rubin, Eve Kosofsky Sedgwick, Teresa de Lauretis, and Judith Butler, among others.

As de Lauretis argues in her introduction to the special issue, queer theory rejects heterosexuality as reflecting norms for sexuality and casts a vision for more expansive sexualities, framing them as possibilities.

> Queer theorists recast the terms of the discourses they engage to expand or shift their semantic horizons and to rethink the sexual in new ways, elsewhere and other-wise. This elsewhere is not a utopia, an otherworldly or future place and time. It is already here . . . in the differently erotic mappings of the body, and in the imaging and enacting of new forms of community by the other-wise desiring subjects of this queer theory.[3]

Further, queer theory pushes back against the claim of homogeneity in gay and lesbian studies. Much of early gay studies (or gay and lesbian studies) was criticized for centering white gay male experience. De Lauretis argues that

> the term "Queer Theory" was arrived at in an effort to avoid all these fine distinctions [between different types of lesbian and gay experiences] in our discursive protocols, not to adhere to any one of the given terms, not to assume their ideological liabilities, but instead to both transgress and transcend them—or at the very least problematize them.[4]

To "problematize" a concept is to strip away conventional understandings of it. According to queer theorists such as de Lauretis, conventional understandings of what it means to be gay or lesbian need to be stripped away because those understandings are largely based on white gay male experience. Even the inclusion of lesbian experience, while valuable, is viewed as insufficient to represent the diverse experiences of other sexual minorities, especially as race, ethnicity, class, and geography are added to the equation: "The differences made by race in self-representation and identity argue for the necessity to examine, question, or contest the usefulness and/or the limitations of current discourses on lesbian and gay sexualities."[5]

In addition to objecting to an overfocus on white men's experiences in the gay community, queer theory also calls into question how the mainstream gay community seems to create its own norms for being gay or lesbian. Queer theorist David Halperin describes how some LGBTQ+ people become disenchanted with the gay liberation movement due to "a growing awareness that gay life has generated its own disciplinary regimes, its own techniques of normalization, in the form of obligatory haircuts, t-shirts, dietary practices, body piercing, leather accoutrements, and physical exercise."[6] Queer theory sees the establishment of norms, whether they are steeped in heterosexual biases or developed within a gay and lesbian framework, as problematic.[7] Queer theory proposes what it sees as a much more expansive vision for sexuality.

Queer theory also largely rejects the attempts in gay and lesbian politics to be assimilated into culture. Whereas the mainstream gay community has pursued assimilation and acceptance in part by adapting and adopting broader cultural norms, queer theorists argue against any kind of normativity. Recall from chapter 1 that many arguments in the early 1990s and early 2000s regarding the etiology (that is, the cause) of sexual orientation involved scientific claims for a biological basis for a homosexual orientation. For those who reject societal norms altogether, this line of argumentation is mostly counterproductive:

> From a queer theory perspective, arguments for a genetic origin of sexuality are to a very small extent helpful in ensuring that the figure of the body is not forgotten in understanding the motivation for attraction, although importantly the body must be understood

as materialised and sexuality must not be relegated into being seen as the cultural expression of a biological desire to breed that is sometimes expressed rightly and sometimes wrongly.[8]

The arguments from biology were an attempt to assimilate into the broader culture, an approach sometimes referred to as a "liberation" model. Queer theory objected to the liberation model for a number of reasons, most notably because it encouraged assimilating into the dominant culture by virtue of being "just like" heterosexuals. Society's norms would essentially stay the same, simply widening slightly to include gay and lesbian people.

According to queer theorists, the liberation approach to gay politics left untouched many underlying heterosexual normative structures:

> Ultimately, I think what the shift away from a liberation model of gay politics reflects is a deepened understanding of the discursive structures and representational systems that determine the production of sexual meanings, and that micromanage individual perceptions, in such a way as to maintain and reproduce the underpinnings of heterosexist privilege.[9]

Let's circle back, then, to heterosexual norms. In the previous chapter, we discussed twentieth-century attempts to demonstrate that homosexuality was a natural (from nature or "born that way") orientation that a small percentage of people experience. This contrasted sharply with previous conceptualizations of homosexuality as a vice or perversion. These efforts resulted only in moving sexual minorities (as we understand them today) from criminal codes to psychiatric classification. Halperin describes this shift as a move from incarceration in prison to incarceration in a psychiatric hospital.[10] From a queer theory perspective, much more needed to be done to dismantle heterosexual normativity and recognize nonnormative sexualities.

One dismantling that has been important in queer theory is the dismantling of binaries. Chief among the binaries treated as problematic is the heterosexual/homosexual binary, which is deemed inherently homophobic in queer theory.[11] In the heterosexual/homosexual binary, heterosexuality is the normative category. People belong in this category by default; if they do not, they are something other than the norm or standard. Those in the homosexual category are not "a real or determinate class of persons" in their own right; rather, their designation as nonnormative serves to delimit and define them "by negation," by not being heterosexual. The heterosexual/homosexual binary is not a "true pair" but "a hierarchical opposition in which heterosexuality defines itself implicitly by constituting itself as the negation of homosexuality." Heterosexuality is the norm against which homosexuality is compared. According to queer theory, then, homosexuality is not a natural reality but a "constructed reality." The homosexual is the "social misfit," the "unnatural monster," the "moral failure," the "sexual pervert," while the heterosexual is the "social norm," "perfectly natural," "highly laudable."[12]

What's Right with Queer Theory?

In 1985, Elaine Storkey published a book titled *What's Right with Feminism?* In that book, Storkey engages feminist theory and identifies contributions from feminism that Christians should engage and understand, even if they have misgivings about other elements of some forms of feminism. We would like to offer a similar engagement with queer theory.

We are both trained in the integration of psychology and theology. Integration entails repositioning psychology in a Christian worldview.[13] Part of the process of repositioning is to engage theories in mainstream psychology. We believe that through natural revelation, God gives people insights into a wide range of subjects that can be engaged and brought into a meaningful dialogue with Christian concepts. In order to do this, Christians must cultivate the virtue of intellectual humility. That is, we must see what a theorist or theory gets right before we move to critique. We want to give people the benefit of the doubt and recognize that God can lead people to helpful insights, even if we do not agree with everything their perspective offers. We also must remain humble about our understanding of Christianity, biblical and systematic theology, spiritual formation, and so on. It is in that spirit that we ask, What can Christians learn from queer theory? As we consider what's right with queer theory, we have to ask, How can we distinguish the tenets of queer theory from a Christian understanding of the human person?

There are a few things that stand out to us as we read queer theorists. These include the potential value in scrutinizing prevailing conventions, recognizing the complexities of the constituted self, appreciating the diversity found within the LGBTQ+ community, accounting for the effects of behavior on our sense of self and personhood, attuning to those on the margins, having empathy for those navigating the closet, having humility about the term "heterosexuality" as a social construct, and repositioning the "art of life" discussion on a Christian worldview.

Scrutinize Prevailing Conventions

One of the strengths of queer theory broadly and Foucault more specifically is the call to scrutinize society's prevailing conventions. Those prevailing assumptions come from various sources of authority and shape our understanding of ourselves and of the meaning and purpose of life.

While the two of us reject the claim that the best way to scrutinize prevailing conventions is through the lens of power relations, we see the value in considering power among many other societal dynamics. We are also not interested in dismantling normative structures, although Christians are always interested in reforming society, identifying sources of injustice so that they continually invite the world around them to help form a more just society.

Queer theory rejects any claim that knowledge is universal or objective. While the two of us don't agree with this assertion, we do recognize how humans sometimes underestimate the shaping influence of sociocultural and historical factors on conjectural knowledge. We can see this influence in the history of the terms "homosexuality" and "heterosexuality," as well as in the movement from religious to psychiatric conceptualizations of homosexuality, the removal of homosexuality from the diagnostic manual, the rise of the mainstream LGBTQ+ community in society, and so many other developments. What all of us have in front of us—what we know about any given topic and how we describe it—is shaped considerably by historical and sociocultural factors that we may not fully appreciate or understand.

As a caution in our critical engagement with queer theory on this first point, we would add that scrutinizing prevailing conventions can lead to a kind of cynicism, a distrust of all structures of authority in society and a corresponding tendency to impute bad motives to others. This can create an unhealthy cynicism that ultimately detracts from or even destroys spiritual growth. Asking good questions and seeking intellectual honesty is one thing; constant scrutiny, distrust, and cynicism for its own sake is another. G. K. Chesterton references this idea when he offers, "The object of opening the mind, as of opening the mouth, is to shut it again on something solid."[14] To scrutinize and mistrust for its own sake can leave one in a state of great instability. More than that, it is the path of the Christian to find solid ground in our faith, even while we continue to wrestle with God in our walk with him.

It is worth noting as well that nobody can ever know absolutely the motivation of another. When queer theorists assume malintent from sources of power and authority in an absolute way, they seem to reflect an unreasonably high degree of confidence in assessing the motivations of others. Dialogue or humble listening for understanding appear to be less valuable for queer theorists in light of the power-based motives that they assume always to be present and threatening.

Recognize the Complexities of the Constituted Self

Foucault reminds us that we are complex subjects and that many forces and experiences contribute to who we understand ourselves to be. For Foucault, much of what shapes us is tied to efforts to control and wield power through language.

We find it helpful to acknowledge that, at times, language can be wielded as a source of power. After all, it's well understood that manipulation can occur at the level of human discourse. However, to frame the forces and experiences that shape our lives as tied broadly to problematic power and authority fails to account for understandings of God's sovereignty and power as good news, not merely oppressive forces.

For the Christian, it seems a reasonable claim that we are constituted not only by language but by a wide array of forces that influence us. At the same time, as complex beings with an intellect and will, we are not merely passive subjects to these forces. A distinctively Christian contribution to this discussion would also account for the ways humans can, with God's help, discern forces and experiences that shape us and be redeemed in the midst of these many forces and experiences without having to dismantle language and norms as such.

Further, it's worth acknowledging that queer theory, and the way it seeks to dismantle linguistic categories and redefine norms, is drawing from the power and influence it has gained to do so. The queer theorist is not exempt from operating within and engaging power dynamics in the reshaping of language. Queer theorists who see themselves as previously without power might consider it equitable, not hypocritical, to seize the power of language formation from the previously dominant group and wield that power for the same purpose. We will discuss the reshaping of language and its impact more explicitly in chapter 3.

Appreciate the Diversity Within the LGBTQ+ Community

We appreciate how queer theory challenges a more restricted understanding of the gay community as largely gay or lesbian, largely white, and largely homogeneous. The layers of complexity queer theory has added to our understanding of the LGBTQ+ community—including differences in race, socioeconomic status, and geographic region—are helpful contributions Christians can recognize and benefit from, even as we push back against some of the postmodern assumptions out of which queer theory emerged.

In fact, one of the ways faithful Christians have found a voice for themselves within the LGBTQ+ community is through the recognition of intersecting identities. Many Christians are navigating questions of faith and sexual identity. The intersection of religious identity and sexual identity is a salient aspect of their sense of self. In his doctoral thesis, David Bennett engages queer theory to make the case that celibate gay Christians essentially "queer the queer." In other words, he writes, these Christians "uncover the bodily practices, affects, and realities of queer pilgrims (i.e., nonrepressive gay celibacy) which have been missed by mainstream (queer) norms and apologetics."[15]

It is, then, important to realize that some conservative Christians view themselves as part of the LGBTQ+ community, however tangentially. They have shared characteristics of same-sex attractions and perhaps other personality characteristics that they see within the community. Some Christians adopt the language of the LGBTQ+ community in terms of self-identifying attributions ("I am a celibate gay Christian" or "I am a Side B gay Christian"). In a sense, queer theory creates a space for them, even though much of queer theory would wish to dismantle the very Christianity that anchors their faith and is such an important part of their intersectional experience.

Account for the Effects of Behavior

Much of Butler's work on gender and sexuality concerns how human traits are not essential categories but performed behaviors. For example, Butler writes, "Gender reality is performative which means, quite simply, that it is real only to the extent that it is performed."[16] For Butler, this performance creates gender through various acts, speech, and behavior. She challenges the idea that gender "expresses or externalizes . . . an objective ideal to which gender aspires; because gender is not a fact."[17] It's worth noting that I (Julia) have heard youth quote Butler's ideas of gender as performative without ever realizing who they are quoting.

We disagree with the claim that gender is merely performative. We see gender as tethered to the sexed body, which is a biological reality reflected in chromosomes, gonads, and genitalia. Gender is expressed socially and culturally, but it is also linked to a given reality outside of social and cultural performance.

Still, we recognize that the way we behave can have an impact on how we perceive ourselves. Further, as we behave in certain ways, or refrain from behaving in other ways, this can certainly shape the person we "become." Even the way we talk about ourselves can shape our sense of self over time. And this can also impact one's experience of gender and sexuality. At the same time, to assert that this process negates the reality of sex distinctions as such would depart from a Christian lens. Chapter 3 will engage with how we might account for the interaction between behavior and one's sense of identity, even as we differentiate our understanding of this interaction from Butler's work.

We also recognize the value in our daily rhythms (or liturgies) of life and how they shape us over time. Queer theory and Butler specifically see us enacting a world around us, by which Butler means we live the norms around us. Queer theorists call people to live and act in ways that upend those norms. Such upending can happen through activist behaviors but also just living one's life as a queer person and pushing back against norms and assumptions. Christians, too, wish to be more aware of the ways in which our habits form us over time. We also want to acknowledge the way certain habits and default patterns can be problematic.

James K. A. Smith has written extensively about this, encouraging Christians to distinguish thin and thick habits and to be intentional about the thick or meaningful habits—habits tied to transcendent reality—that are tied to our faith, how God is working in our lives, and who God is calling us to be. Likewise, Christians are to identify cultural liturgies and how they shape us; we are to create counterliturgies in our own lives and in our own communities that shape us in ways we are meant to be shaped.[18]

It's worth asking, What contributes to the liturgies offered to youth today? As we suggested in chapter 1, digital and social media are the stages on which much of sexual identity is being performed. While we disagree with Butler that gender is real only insofar as it is performed, we want to critically engage the ways digital and social media provide contexts for the cocreation of emerging sexual and gender identities. In other words, if we wish to look at liturgies, we have to consider how digital and social media function for young people in a liturgical fashion.

Rob Cover defines digital interactivity as "the capacity for users to generate, share and manipulate content." Digital interactivity has "radically shifted how we engage with the kinds of knowledge frameworks we depend upon to produce and perform coherent and intelligible identities."[19] What happens in digital and social media, in part, is that young people engage in "identity work" by "maintaining profiles, telling stories from [their] everyday life, indicating [their] attitudes and preferences towards politics or popular culture, connecting with other people, uploading selfies and other images and so on."[20]

A question that arises in digital and social media is whether the identity a user communicates exists prior to digital interactivity or whether that identity is created or cocreated in those forums. Cover observes that the earliest social networks assumed a reality and self that posted online (say, to Facebook) and essentially returned to "real life."[21]

What Cover does in drawing on Butler and queer theory is ask to what extent young people perform their identities. He considers how "what [they] do in the face of others is not merely a representation that may be more-or-less the same as [their] core selves but actually forms that core self through repetitive practices."[22] That is, when youth are active online, he points out, there is a dynamic relationship between the self they reflect and the self they become, mediated by the very engagement and adoption of norms they see and then display on media.

Youth who identify with emerging sexual identities may do "identity work" in digital and social media and cocreate identity in a social milieu of their peers. Cover raises valid concerns about how digital interactions and social media engagement can lead to "identity incoherence and unintelligibility" despite being "one of the most powerful accounts of the complexity . . . of identity and self-hood."[23] We would share his observation that these platforms are not neutral in impacting the youth navigating them and often play an active role in shaping these youth. Even still, we believe that if social media is the primary place for reflecting and shaping identity and community, it will leave us wanting.

Interestingly, queer theory raises similar questions many Christians have about social media from a different worldview and set of assumptions. We can disagree with the worldview and set of assumptions while acknowledging points of shared knowledge and understanding. To what extent can identity be performed on and thus shaped by social media? To what extent is that performance powerful in its impact on the expansion of emerging sexual identities? In asking these questions, it seems plausible that people sometimes become the thing they act like.

Attune to Those on the Margins

Queer theory reminds us to attune to those on the margins. Butler's claim about norms, according to Cover, is that norms are often "problematic and regimentary and often in ways which unethically exclude some subjects from being recognized as subjects or having the opportunity to lead a fully liveable life."[24] Norms "act on us," according to Butler. Cover observes that this occurs "in a way that makes all subjects vulnerable, and *unevenly* vulnerable." It is not that straight people are the problem; rather, it is that straightness is being supported as the norm and "heterosexuality as the *sole legitimate sexual identity and practice*."[25] As we noted above, in a fallen world, norms can contribute to inequality in society. Christians can recognize the existence of nonnormative, emerging sexual identities and decide what posture to take in seeing and caring for those who have nonnormative experiences.

We attempted to do this, for example, in a study of celibate gay Christians, a group that is on the margins of both the mainstream LGBTQ+ community and the conservative Christian community. In our study of three hundred celibate gay Christians, we interviewed a number of participants to understand how they saw their unique gifts as a blessing to others within the church. One theme that emerged was that celibate gay Christians see themselves as more likely to be attuned to those on the margins. For example, Charles shared:

> If it hadn't been for this, this long, drawn-out experience of suffering and processing suffering and what that is like. Like, I wouldn't have at all been able to relate to marginalized people or people who are really lost and alone. . . . And I have found that many times it is really my experience of my spirituality that gives me the compassion, and often it gives me some sort of way into the conversation,

or some sort of way that I can begin to have empathy for people. And I really think that it has made me so much softer and compassionate and really given me the heart of Christ.[26]

Another celibate gay Christian, Alex, shared something similar: "If I had no minority status at all, I don't think I would be—[I] wouldn't have that empathy for marginalized people if I wasn't marginalized."[27]

As Christians, we disagree with queer theory's claim that norms are necessarily a source of oppression that creates and maintains margins. Inequality and marginalization are the result of many forces in society; most of all, they are a consequence of evil and sin. How norms are articulated, how they are held, and whether they are weaponized can contribute to marginalization and inequality, but norms do not have to be articulated or held in these manners, nor do they need to be weaponized.

Norms have been and continue to be orienting principles across cultures and time and space. Even while queer theory argues for the removal of norms, this antinormativity also becomes its own established pattern (norm) that can lead to marginalizations within and between groups. That is, the rejection of norms can create its own set of norms. Further, the queer theorist is not less prone to marginalizing others merely by acknowledging other groups who have the capacity to marginalize, any more than the Christian is less prone to sin by identifying the sins of others. What queer theory fails to recognize is something Christians affirm: that all of us are sinful people. Even our best intentions are limited by the fallen reality around us and within us. It is the life of grace that works in us and transforms our hearts to more readily see the "other" as God sees them.

Have Empathy for Those Navigating the Closet

Sexual minorities often refer to a time at which they were "in the closet," a time of secrecy in which they hid their sexuality from others. Queer theory reminds us of the dilemma the closet represents. This observation is not unique to queer theory, but it is one that queer theorists have thoughtfully engaged. Reflecting on Eve Kosofsky Sedgwick's *Epistemology of the Closet*, David Halperin observes,

> The closet is an impossibly contradictory place: you can't be in it, and you can't be out of it. You can't be in it because—so long as you are in the closet—you can never be certain of the extent to which you have actually succeeded in keeping your homosexuality secret. After all, one effect of being in the closet is that you are precluded from knowing whether people are treating you as straight because you have managed to fool them and they do not suspect you of being gay, or whether they are treating you as straight because they are playing along with you and enjoying the epistemological privilege that your ignorance of their knowledge affords them.[28]

Halperin, expounding on Sedgwick, highlights the real predicament of a person navigating being in the closet and a person outside of it. On the one hand, being in the closet can lead to profound angst about whether people know or are merely pretending until a disclosure occurs. This level of scrupulosity and the many efforts to act in a way that would not lead to suspicion coexist with the desire to be known. This often can lead to a tipping point where disclosure occurs. At the same time, a person faces challenges when they come out of the closet:

> Those who have once enjoyed the epistemological privilege constituted by their knowledge of your ignorance of their knowledge typically refuse to give up that privilege, and insist on constructing your sexuality as a secret to which they have special access, a secret which always gives itself away to their superior and knowing gaze.[29]

In addition, the person in the closet can come out only too soon or too late, as Halperin sees it. If they come out too soon, they are met with either "impatient dismissal," accused of unnecessarily flaunting their sexuality, or with indifference. If they come out too late, they face the accusation (from themself or others) that if they had been honest with themself, they would have come out earlier.[30] An added insight from queer theory, according to Halperin, is that the closet is both interpersonal (how others know you) and institutional (what is allowable in organizations and institutions). Distinguishing between the interpersonal and the institutional is certainly important in Christian organizations, including churches, parachurch ministries, and education.

Many Christians do not appreciate the power of the closet and the shame that grows in secrecy. The evangelical Christian subculture, in particular, often contributes to this shame when it treats gay people with a level of disgust simply because of their same-sex attractions. When Christians suggest that gay people's attractions are the result of willful disobedience rather than something that they "find themselves" experiencing, we contribute to keeping them closeted, building an environment where shame grows more and more.

The reader may be wondering whether the closet applies in the same way to emerging sexual identities and microminoritized sexual and gender identities. The closet is not likely identical to experiences of being gay or transgender from the dominant taxonomy. We have shared throughout this book how much of identity is cocurated in digital and social media, as young people try on social identities. However, the underlying attractions or experiences of gender may still be kept hidden from others, particularly parents or those in the church. There can be a compartmentalization in making partial disclosures (e.g., online) while remaining closeted at home or at youth group. We should still be attuned to the challenges young people face in navigating their experiences of sexuality and gender, labels used to convey emerging sexual and gender identities (both privately to themselves and publicly to others), and the family and communities of which they are a part.

We both have spent years hearing the stories of people who felt they could not share what they were experiencing with others, who lived for years wondering what people would "really think" of them if they knew this part of their experience. There is something remarkably healthy about being honest about what one experiences, and finding a way to share this reality puts a person in a much better position to respond to their situation.

With teens adopting emergent categories, the closet can look a bit different. Some teens will be trying on various identities with peers or through social media while not sharing this experience with their youth minister or parents. So, while the teens may seem free from shame in their open disclosure of identities and shifting in and out of various labels, especially in online forums, they might be missing out on the intimacy that comes from in-person relationships with trusted adults who can offer support, validation, and care. These teens may not even see themselves as closeted and might fail to appreciate what they are missing by bracketing out this aspect of their experience from their primary relationships with parents and other mentors. They, too, may carry shame, but it would be easy to assume they don't, and therefore parents or ministers might miss an opportunity to attend to the vulnerabilities and fears that they are carrying.

Humbly Recognize That Heterosexuality Is a Social Construct

Queer theory also reminds us that just as "homosexuality" is a social construct, so too is the term "heterosexuality." As we stated in chapter 1, prior to the nineteenth century people could describe the experiences and practices that today constitute heterosexuality—they experienced attraction toward people of the opposite sex, and some would engage in sexual behaviors as an expression of attraction—but they did not have the language for what today we refer to as "heterosexual" or "heterosexuality" or think of sexuality in terms of identity.

We would offer that queer theory challenges the inherent goodness and inerrancy some Christians assume in heterosexuality. This critique is one we share, given that Christians have, at times, forgotten how heterosexuality also includes the propensity toward lust and how some opposite-sex relationships would also not align with God's plan for human sexuality. Within a Christian framework, each person's sexuality is touched by the fall—in other words, all of our sexualities can be disordered in the sense that they order us in ways that fall short of God's ideal. This is not less true for the heterosexually oriented person who experiences lust.

Reposition the "Art of Life" Discussion on a Christian Worldview

Foucault's writing about ethics and personal transformation as a "style of life" and "art of life" suggests an entryway into what we believe can be a productive posture for discussion and ministry. When Foucault wrote about a style of life or an art of life, he seems to have in mind people whose ethics are rooted not in laws or shared moral codes but in "practices of the self"; as Marli Huijer explains, "Morality was not pre-given, but came into being in self-practices."[31] In other words, ethics had to be continually discerned and renegotiated in relation to the developing practices of the individual's life.

We don't share the stark individualism of Foucault's formulation, nor would we prefer that personal rules of conduct and societal moral codes oppose one another. Christians have long been drawn to concepts that see personal and societal conduct as developing side by side and shaping one another, such as the "rule of life" developed by St. Benedict, which cast a vision for living for oneself *and* for community.

At the same time, we want to honor that Foucault brings forward the relevance of ongoing reflection and discernment in the particulars of our individual lives and experiences when it comes to parsing out difficult ethical and moral dilemmas. We do find value in the idea that morality and ethics are not one-time considerations. Further, we would offer that laws and shared moral codes in a society, in and of themselves, are not exhaustive in leading to moral living.

We want to build on Foucault's assertion of the value of a style of life that can orient us and involves ongoing practices that take shape over time. We appreciate Jay Johnson's reflections as a queer Christian theologian when he builds upon an "art of life" perspective to depict the significance of God's active and ongoing work in a person's life:

> Regardless of sexuality, gender, race, ethnicity, intelligence, or any other marker in social classification schemes, "God made me this way" fails as a good theological claim. The past tense in that claim demands revision in our theological reflection for a more lively and dynamic insight: "God *is making* me in a particular way," and not only with my help but also in concert with a community of others for a project currently underway and far from over. That "project" is you, me, all of us together.[32]

This integrative engagement with Foucault's personal "art of life" leaves room for us to consider God's active work in the life of the believer and through a community of brothers and sisters in Christ. We will unpack this much more in part 2 of this book. For now, we want to lean into a critique of queer Christian theology to round out our engagement with queer theory.

Although we find value in queer theory, it is not the only way to scrutinize prevailing conventions, recognize the complexities of the constituted self, appreciate the diversity found within the LGBTQ+ community, account for the effects of behavior on our sense of self and personhood, attune to those on the margins, have empathy for those navigating the closet, show humility about the term "heterosexuality" as a social construct, and engage in the "art of life." Each of these areas can be addressed through other theories, including a Christian worldview that speaks to emerging sexual identities.

What About Queer Christian Theology?

Queer theology is the application of queer theory to theology. Queer Christian theology applies queer theory to Christian biblical studies, hermeneutics, systematic theology, and so on. For example, Linn Marie Tonstad's book *God and Difference* engages and critiques trinitarian theology from a queer theology perspective. Similar to what we saw in queer theory's criticism of mainstream LGBTQ+ liberation strategies, queer Christian theology is not focused on getting LGBTQ+ people a place at the table of Christian faith through tolerance and affirmation; rather, queer Christian theology scrutinizes the table itself, challenging the accepted norms of Christianity.[33]

What we appreciate about people drawn to queer Christian theology is the desire to disentangle Christianity from the cultural knots that may be far too familiar to us to even notice. Queer theologian Jay Johnson observes that much of contemporary Christianity is deeply influenced by modern Western classifications that can obscure our seeing the gospel and applying it to the needs of society today. Insofar as our Christian faith is viewed through the lens of the sociocultural context in which it is embedded, what we believe to be true and possible is affected. "The question at hand ... turns not on *whether* Christian faith shapes our perceptions but *what* it invites into our field of vision."[34] This is an important reminder for Christians in all cultures and throughout history to reflect on the historical and cultural settings that serve as a backdrop to our reading and application of Scripture. Johnson correctly reminds us of the unique historical context and events that led to the creation of the categories "homosexuality" and "heterosexuality," as we discussed in chapter 1. Christians ought to acknowledge and keep in view the ways historical context, social context, and access to language and categories are reflected in our understanding and expression of Christian faith.

A distinction we want to make between our understanding and queer theology is the differing views of ancient societies' influence on the Scriptures. Queer theologians are right to remind us of the sociocultural contexts in which books of the Bible were written, including the hierarchical terms that were present in many of those societies and are present to varying degrees in Scripture. Queer theologians call for us to disentangle those assumptions from our reading. Our concern with adopting queer theology is that we see in it a failure to appreciate God's providential work in recording what needed to be recorded for a canon of Scripture to be made available to those who follow Christ. While we agree that the Bible has several important cultural contexts, we also believe in God's sovereignty and providence in bringing together what was necessary for God's Word to be available to the world.

Queer Christian theologians, when reflecting on hermeneutics and biblical interpretation, encourage us to "let the text breathe" rather than impose one singular and "correct" interpretation that all must adhere to: "The goal . . . will not turn on 'getting it right' but instead on 'getting it better,' when we judge 'better' based on how much thriving and abundant life a particular reading generates for all."[35] We are drawn to the idea of letting the text breathe, and we do invite the Holy Spirit to impress upon us what God has for us in the reading of his Word. At the same time, we also uphold the concept of a canon of Scripture and a shared understanding of the meaning of the text (usually understood in creedal statements expressing the basics of orthodoxy) that can be passed down over generations and shared across cultures. We suggest that both of these ways to read Scripture can stand together. Letting the text breathe and affirming a canonical understanding are not adversaries but may be helpful companions when used by the Spirit.

Related to the topics of hermeneutics and biblical interpretation, queer Christian theology has a fairly limited range of interpretive strategies, relying primarily on skeptical critique and on what Tonstad calls "suspicious reading."[36] While we see some value in the critiques of queer theory, we believe intellectual humility is a more compelling virtue than cynicism. We have found that cynicism can lead to the death of spiritual vitality and of intellectual and relational generosity.

Queer theology is critical of natural theology, of the idea that we can look to nature to help us understand norms that God established. As Johnson puts it, "Historically, religion has intervened into this perplexing line of questioning with a deceptively simple claim: nature means whatever God intends. Deviating from that divine intent constitutes an unnatural act, and religion provides not only the means to know what God intends but also to ensure the manifestation of that intent in practice."[37] This is probably where we have one of our sharper disagreements with queer theology. We see nature as instructive when we relate general revelation and special revelation. Whereas queer theology is "deeply suspicious"[38] of nature, we want to be careful in our examination of nature without becoming as deeply suspicious as queer theologians do.

Queer Christian theologians rightly remind us of the value of diversity in community: "Queer people can detect rather astutely, for example, when the rush to conformity signals a fear of difference, the fear of those 'others' whose language, culture, perspective, and relationships seem to threaten cherished assumptions and worldviews."[39] This is an important insight, but one that can be achieved apart from queer theory. The multiethnic church movement in the United States, for instance, reflects the value of diversity in reminding us that heaven will be a place in which people from every tongue, tribe, and nation praise God (Rev. 7:9–10). The value of diversity is not only for the heavenly gathering in that beautiful Revelation image; the multiethnic church is a great exhorter for inclusion and confrontation of othering too.

Queer theologians also seek to promote a high view of the body and embodied existence. As an extension of that position, they view sexual desire as instructive and "a source of insight."[40] Our view is that Christianity itself holds a high view of embodied existence. While there have been times in our history when we followers of Christ have devalued the body and elevated the spirit, a proper Christian understanding values both body and spirit. Desire, too, is instructive. Our longing for completion in the other (eros) is intended to remind us that we will only approximate that completion in sexual intimacy and behavior. Christian tradition has long viewed sexuality as a profound gift from a loving Creator, but it is a gift that points to an even greater reality. True satisfaction of our desire and longing for completion will come when we as a bride (the church) are joined with the bridegroom (Jesus) in the consummation of all things.

The application of queer theology to gender and transgender experiences has been presented as a journey and discovery of the self.[41] Queer Christian theologian Justin Sabia-Tanis likens his discovery of his gender identity to the discovery of a vocation: "Gender differences arise in response to our following of God's leading for our individual lives. God calls some people to go on a journey that may include a change of gender, a transformative pilgrimage."[42] Such a view reflects to some extent Butler's claim that gender is performed and that one becomes one's gender.[43] While we disagree that the sum of gender is its performance, we recognize that how people behave as gendered persons shapes their sense of identity. However, we believe God intended from creation that gender be tethered to sex. While there may be exceptions to this norm—experiences in which gender does not appear tethered to sex—such experiences are exceptions that point to the norm rather than calls for the deconstruction of that norm.

Although we agree with queer Christian theologians in some ways, we believe that queer theory is not essential to reach the same conclusions. Valuing diversity and our embodied existence, for example, can be achieved apart from queer theory. Meanwhile, the areas where we disagree with queer Christian theologians do not compel us to shift our understandings as Christians toward queer theology.

Of particular importance to ministers and parents considering queer theology and queer theory is that queer theory leaves no place for authoritative revelation or for divine law. Within queer theory, everything is open to deconstruction. That is one of the consequences of its antinormative stance. In that way, queer theology and orthodoxy are at odds, by definition. Orthodoxy implies a norm, a rule of faith, whereas queer theory is antinorm.[44]

Concluding Thoughts

We have already acknowledged that while queer theory is incredibly influential on today's youth and the emerging landscape of sexual identities, most youth are not aware of the power of this influence on self-understanding. The point of continuity between queer theory and emergent taxonomies is queer theory's deconstruction of sexual difference as a stable, natural binary. That assumption underlies both versions.

The theory underlying the emergent sexual identity taxonomies at times contradicts queer theory in meaningful ways. Within emerging sexual identities, there is a move toward hypercategorization. Conversely, queer theory is about dismantling categories, not creating and monitoring new ones. This can lead to contention between, on the one hand, those who see hypercategorization as a delimiting way to control language and demand unhelpful precision and, on the other hand, those who see these categorizations as freeing. Additionally, queer theory sees gender as a construct that is (1) outside of the self; (2) artificial; and (3) oppressive. Thus, the goal is to "queer" and deconstruct these and all categories. Today's prominent theory within emergent taxonomies presents sexual orientation and gender identity categories as indicative of something (1) intrinsic to the self; (2) deeply real or essential (i.e., who I "really am"); and (3) liberating. These are just a few of the apparent contradictions within the emergent categories. In some ways, emergent categories have queer theory to thank for their existence, but they depart from queer theory in key ways that are worth acknowledging and engaging with.

As we bring this chapter to a close, we will work to illuminate the dynamics at play that move beyond queer theory. For this, we want to turn to Ian Hacking, his distinction between human kinds and natural kinds, and the concept of looping effects, to gain a better understanding for how sexual identities come into being alongside changes in the theory, language, and categories for understanding them.

This will offer the final piece of conceptual grounding before we turn to part 2 and consider effective ministry and parenting to youth so shaped by the theoretical foundations we are laying in part 1.

CHAPTER 3

How Sexual Identities Come into Being

"I would've thought of myself as gay until I realized there are so many other options available to me," fourteen-year-old Daniella shared. "I've been wondering about how I account for the people I could be attracted to, without boxing myself into one type of person, and I think I found something that fits. I've been trying to learn more about the labels out there, because I want to figure it out. Sure, up until now I pretty much had crushes on girls, but who knows what will happen next."

Daniella speaks to what some of our teen clients are highlighting. The changing landscape of language and categories impacts the youth interacting with this landscape. Parents are trying to figure out how to understand the landscape and respond to language that activates in themselves a range of reactions.

Daniella's parents sat with me soon after Daniella shared with them about her exploration of sexual identity labels. "We don't even know where to begin," they reflected. Daniella's parents, like many other Christian parents, shared that they "know gay people but can't wrap our mind around what Daniella is saying." They had a range of questions for me:

- "Where did this type of language come from?"
- "Is Daniella getting negatively influenced by her friends?"
- "How do we not shut her down? We are glad she is talking to us, but we don't want to pretend we understand what we don't understand. We want to be honest about the concerns we have about this language and the pressure she seems to feel to come up with a label because her friends are labeling themselves."

FOR PARENTS: STAY ENGAGED

Much of emergent language is being "tried on" in online forums and contexts in ways that understandably concern parents. Peers certainly can affect how a teen comes to think of themselves and the language and categories they are drawn to. We want to dissuade teens from absorbing the ideas of others without thoughtfully engaging with those ideas. But simply telling a teen that their peers are a bad influence does little good. It often seems to alienate the teen from their parents. We recommend that parents be invested in knowing the young people their teen is friends with, identifying unhealthy dynamics when present, and refraining from criticizing a friend simply because they identify with emergent categories.

Being genuine is part of a healthy relationship and true validation. So, if a parent conceals their questions or concerns about emerging sexual identities, it doesn't foster a strong, secure bond. Healthy relationships can endure questions and concerns. We recommend parents keep talking with their teen about what they are drawn to in those labels. Get the teen talking about what resonates for them about the term. But don't stop there. Invite the teen to share questions and concerns they have about labeling. Parents can acknowledge the challenge of navigating these labels, especially at such a young age. Parents need not pretend they have no questions or concerns. We want to encourage parents to find ways to invite a teen to explore these concerns in a dialogue, not a lecture.

We want in this chapter to better understand the challenges families like Daniella's are facing. We'll do this by exploring how language and categories change in response to the experiences of those who are categorized. When we categorize people as gay or lesbian, bicurious or on the ace spectrum, we open up ways for youth to think about themselves and their sexual identity as well as open up new ways for them to behave and think about their history. We will explore to what extent people "come into existence" through classifications and to what extent these classifications change the people who are classified. To do so, let's begin with the looping effect.

The Looping Effect

In *Emerging Gender Identities*, we discussed the work of Ian Hacking and his concept of a "looping effect." We argued that the looping effect offers a good explanation for the recent rise in emerging gender identities. In this chapter, we draw once more on Hacking and apply his idea of a looping effect to emerging sexual identities.

According to Hacking, a looping effect is an ongoing and mutually influential dynamic that exists between groups of people and categories for groups of people in the human sciences.[1] To state it succinctly, the looping effect describes how changes in ideas about people end up changing people and how groups of people who have changed force those around them to think about them differently.[2]

The notion of the looping effect originated from Hacking's experience studying demography and his observation that people respond to how they are categorized. Of course, we all interact with language and categories that shape our experience of ourselves and the world around us. But Hacking is particularly interested in how people change their behavior and self-conceptualization in response to how they are categorized.[3]

Hacking observes that mental health classifications and diagnoses are one significant way in which people are categorized in our society. When we look at diagnostic classifications, we see that disorders come and go, and they do so in the context of a changing society. We have seen many disorders removed from or added to the diagnostic manual; mental health classifications are hardly etched in stone. While a lot goes into adding and removing diagnoses, Hacking draws our attention to how people react to and change their behavior in response to changes in diagnostic categorization. Diagnoses change in response to society, of course, but people seem to also change their behaviors in ways that align with certain diagnoses.

There is an ongoing interaction, then, between mental health experts who make diagnoses, broader societal views about what constitutes a mental health concern, experts who determine which diagnoses accurately account for mental health concerns, and the people who are grouped under a particular diagnosis. According to Hacking, the looping effect involves interaction between five entities (see fig. 3.1): (1) classification, (2) the people, (3) institutions, (4) knowledge, and (5) experts:

1. *Classification* is a grouping of some kind. Whenever we assign people to groups or categories, we are classifying them. Diagnoses are one specific way we classify people. As we add new classifications, including diagnoses, new types of people are created. Think of the person who suffers from schizophrenia ("the schizophrenic") or the person who is thought to have a same-sex sexual orientation or engages in same-sex sexual behavior ("the homosexual"). Hacking explains, "To create new ways of classifying people is also to change how we can think of ourselves, to change our sense of self-worth, even how we remember our own past. This in turn generates a looping effect, because people of the kind behave differently and so are different. That is to

say the kind changes, and so there is new causal knowledge to be gained and perhaps, old causal knowledge to be jettisoned."[4]

2. *The people* refers to those being grouped, categorized, or classified. In the mental health field, the "people" refers to patients or clients who receive a diagnosis. As we noted above, the people being classified are aware that they are being classified and may change their behavior and their way of understanding themselves in response to how they are classified. For instance, what we refer to today as the transgender community at one time rejected the way they were being classified (receiving mental health diagnoses as transsexual or as having a transvestic fetish) in favor of a political and public identity as transgender.

3. *Institutions* (including meetings, societies, and other gatherings) are entities that arise to listen to, research, and understand the experiences of the people who have been classified. Institutions rework theories as people respond to how they have been classified. As people change their behavior and their understanding of themselves, research and theory adapt to understand those experiences better.

4. *Knowledge* refers to what constitutes shared understanding of the people being classified in a society. Hacking sometimes refers to this shared understanding as "conjectural knowledge," because it may be somewhat speculative. This knowledge is shared and passed along in society at the level of popular culture. It reflects taken-for-granted ways of thinking about a topic or people group.

5. *Experts* are those people and organizations granted a certain status in society that allows them to determine what counts as actual knowledge (not conjecture or speculation) about the people being classified. Experts also determine how knowledge should be used in applied settings. Mainstream

mental health organizations, for instance, represent a collection of experts who develop position papers, guidelines, and policies on human kinds that are classified with reference to diagnostic nosology (classification of mental health concerns, in this instance). Outstanding questions and controversies are settled by experts. This brings the loop back to classification: Human kinds are "modified, revised classifications are formed, and the classified change again, loop upon loop."[5]

To help explain a looping effect, Hacking distinguishes between *natural kinds* and *human kinds*. Natural kinds, such as chemical compounds, do not react to their scientific categorization. Human

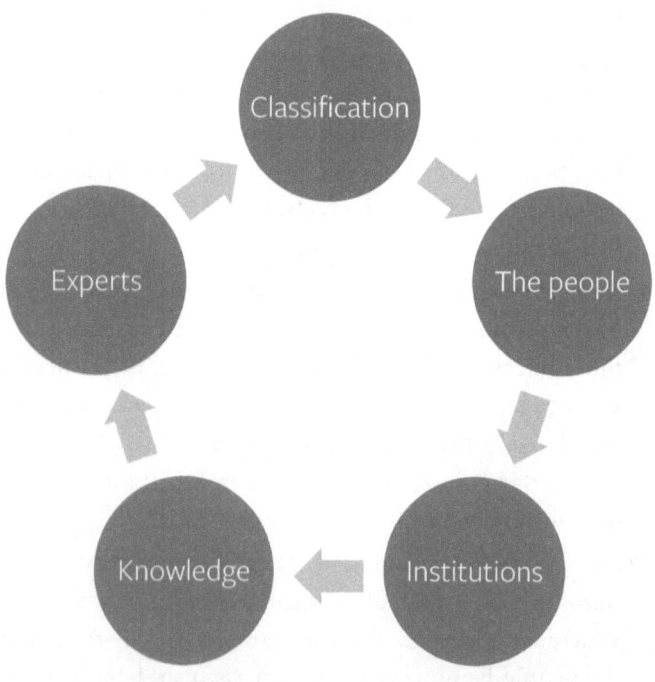

Figure 3.1 The looping effect

kinds, in contrast, do react to how they are grouped or categorized. Here is how Hacking describes these reactions:

> The dynamics of human kinds is fascinating. Let a new way to classify human beings emerge, and let people become aware of how they are classified, then they will often behave differently (not necessarily better or worse, but differently). The truths about that category of people will change because the people have changed. In consequence, the classifications may themselves have to be modified, for what is being classified has changed. Certainly the knowledge that the classifications are used to encode will change. That is, classifications interact with the classified.[6]

As we noted above, a primary way we classify people in society is through diagnostic nomenclature: The schizophrenic person. The masochistic person. The autistic person. When mental health professionals or organizations identify mental health categories, people who are affected by their categorization interact with how they have been categorized. Like any other category, a mental health category affects how people think about themselves, including how they think about their behavior, identity, and history.[7]

Hacking gives another example: the autistic child. He says,

> By my criteria, "the autistic child" is a human kind. It became a cutting-edge kind [a kind that is current and culturally salient] in the 1970s. The *Journal of Autism and Childhood Schizophrenia* was founded in 1971, and was renamed the *Journal of Autism and Developmental Disorders* in 1979. We are strongly inclined to say that autistic children form a definite class that could, in principle, have been picked out in many populations at many times. We say this because we take it to result from a biological rather than a social deficit. In fact, autism was first characterized by Leo Kanner on the basis of children he noticed in 1938. He thought that they would previously have been called born-deaf or feeble-minded.

He described them in print in *The Nervous Child*, a cutting-edge journal then entering its second year of publication.

The criteria for identification, let alone theories about what autism "is," have changed a good deal since 1938. The optimistic scientific view is that we are establishing a better and better understanding of autism, refining our definition of this natural kind of behaviour and discovering its cause and its essence.[8]

Not only can we trace the history of looping that led to the autistic child, but we can also see how the looping effect led to the classification of Asperger's syndrome for a high-functioning autistic child. After further observation and interaction, Asperger's syndrome was removed from the diagnostic nomenclature, showing how classifications are reworked and refined over time.

Further, those who are classified and their communities respond to the very classifications applied to them. Historically, people with the diagnosis were thought of as very low-functioning individuals who would have poor prognosis, in part because of the limited terminology available. Then, with the emergence of Asperger's, there was space for another category of individuals who could be seen as high functioning and quite bright. People could then be more forthcoming about acknowledging Asperger's than they might if provided with only "autistic" as a category.

Behaviorally, upon a diagnosis of autism, some individuals and their families experience greater withdrawal from others, including their faith community, demonstrating by their behavior a felt sense of alienation in light of this diagnostic classification. Others may today be drawn into online communities of fellow people on the autism spectrum and may invest in new technologies, activities, and resources that are recommended by others in those communities. Still others may be drawn to immerse themselves into particular interests or stimming behaviors tied to their neurodivergence, feeling a freedom to do so in the context of this classification. At times, clinicians also end up assessing people who do not meet criteria for autism but who may be drawn to identify with this community for a variety of reasons, including other symptoms that may overlap with autism.

This is just one example of human kinds that have come into being through the looping effect. Let's now apply our discussion of human kinds and the looping effect to sexuality and sexual orientation.

Looping Effects, Sexual Orientation, and New Meanings of Terms

Hacking reflects on the events surrounding the words "homosexual" and "homosexuality" this way: "The concept 'homosexual,' on my view of history, was once owned by the medical and legal professions. The people categorized as homosexuals took over the ownership of the concept, and changed names, changed meanings, changed the world."[9] These classifications of sexuality are what Hacking elsewhere refers to as "self-ascriptive"[10] kinds; what he means by this is that the people to whom the terms were given changed the meaning of the terms. As a result of this, we have witnessed the emergence and growth of the modern gay community and the new meanings of terms associated with being gay. Hacking elaborates:

> The homosexual as a kind of person emerges in medico-forensic discourse late in the nineteenth century, with instant dispersion.... To simplify overly much, the label "homosexual" was a term in its original sites applied by the knowers to the known. However, it was quickly taken up by the known, and gay liberation was the natural upshot. One of the first features of gay liberation was gay pride and coming out of the closet. It became a moral imperative for people of the kind to identify themselves, to ascribe a chosen kind-term to themselves. That way they also

became the knowers, even if not the only people authorized to have knowledge.[11]

Being self-ascriptive (changing the meaning of terms used to describe a group of people) is related to the distinction Hacking makes between the "knowers" and the "known." The knowers are the experts we noted above, the people who determine what counts as knowledge about a human kind. They determine the classifications. The experts conduct the research. They study those who are known. The known are the very people who are under discussion. They are the ones who are aware that they are being classified, and they interact with the labels used to classify them. They may talk to experts about their experiences. They may also be self-ascriptive: In the case of homosexuality, people who are gay changed the meaning of the words used to account for them, completely upending "gay," which had been a slur, into a point of pride and celebration.[12] Self-ascription allows the known to become knowers.

Let's look at an example of how known people can exercise agency as knowers and become participants in the (re)creation of classification by discussing the history of the words "gay" and "queer," as they are two of the more commonly used self-ascriptive terms, moving from derogatory connotations to positive self-attributions.

History of Terms

The word "gay" originated in the twelfth century in England and derived from the French *gai*, which was derived from a Germanic term. "Gay" originally meant "carefree" or "full of mirth" but was later, in the early seventeenth century, associated with illicit behavior. In the nineteenth century it referred to women who were prostitutes and to men who were sexually promiscuous. In the early twentieth century the word "gay" began to be associated with homosexual people. By the mid-twentieth century, within the gay community, the word "gay" was preferred over the word "homosexual," which was viewed as psychiatric and pathologizing.[13]

There is an agential power among people classified as "homosexual" or "gay" to conceive of themselves in an increasingly positive light. This reflects Hacking's claim that the gay community is self-ascriptive insofar as they have taken a derogatory term and reclaimed it as a positive term for self-identification. Homosexuality would eventually be removed as a diagnostic classification. It took several years to witness the full removal of the classification, but it was eventually removed. The mainstream gay community, as it has emerged as a culture, is then the result of the looping effect for how people have thought about themselves as language changed away from "homosexual" to "gay," and part of these shifts included the removal of homosexuality from the diagnostic nosology of mental health professionals.

Something similar occurred with the word "queer." The word originated as an identity category and slur in the late nineteenth century, probably around the time of the trial of Oscar Wilde in 1895.[14] It was more widely used as a slur against homosexual persons in the early twentieth century. Interestingly, from as early as 1937, the word "queer" has been used within the gay community as a positive term of self-reference.[15] According to Mollie Clarke, the word "queer" would come to suggest a kind of gender and sexual fluidity by the late twentieth and early twenty-first centuries. Today "queer" is commonly used as a positive term that may for some people be synonymous with "gay" and for others be an alternative to the dominant taxonomy of "gay" and represent a nonnormative alternative to sexuality or gender, suggesting a more expansive use of the term. As Clarke observes, "Tracing the history of the word 'Queer' over the last few centuries demonstrates not only the ways in which the term itself has changed—its use and its meaning—but it also highlights societal changes towards gender and sexuality."[16]

So both "gay" and "queer" are examples of derogatory terms that have been reclaimed by the LGBTQ+ community as positive. For Hacking, these are examples of self-ascription. As we have seen, Hacking sees the emergence of "the homosexual" (and later shifts in preference for "gay" and "queer") as reflecting shifts in how people understood themselves due to the looping effect.

The same could be said for "the heterosexual," although there were different dynamics in play for this looping effect. As we saw in chapter 1, the history of heterosexuality involves the use of a designation to account for the context for sexual behaviors ordered toward procreation. Although it would take many years, the term "heterosexual" eventually came to refer to a sexual orientation toward the opposite sex, which would affect how people thought of themselves individually and as a group. Institutions would study heterosexual people, and we would see the emergence of taken-for-granted understandings of heterosexuality. Experts would eventually refine the designation of "heterosexuality" with greater clarity and consensus.

People typically must either think about themselves in relation to how they are categorized or else reject the classification itself. By either expanding or reformulating the language and categories used to describe a phenomenon, people may change or expand the ways they experience themselves and their history. This confirmation or revision is a part of the looping effect. Who we are in relation to how we are categorized depends, in part, on how the grouping or categorization is made available to us.[17]

Once a group of people (in this case, "homosexuals") have been classified, organizations associated with classification arise (see fig. 3.2). These can include professional conferences, professional organizations, and related institutional endeavors such as task forces, working groups, and committees that reflect institutional thought and shape popular thought about a topic. These are not always experts in a directly related field of study but can include people from a range of disciplines. We no longer reference "the homosexual" and are much more likely to speak of the "LGBTQ+ community," a community that has arisen as a culture of sorts that can be accounted for by the looping effect. The changes in popular culture are seen by many as the taken-for-granted realities about the mainstream LGBTQ+ community. There is a sense that this is a culture that has assimilated into broader culture, and anyone who sees it differently is sometimes seen as a problematic minority. Medical and psychological experts weigh in through a range of forums, including social media and broader media platforms, on what counts as knowledge about the LGBTQ+ community and how to best apply that knowledge in various settings.

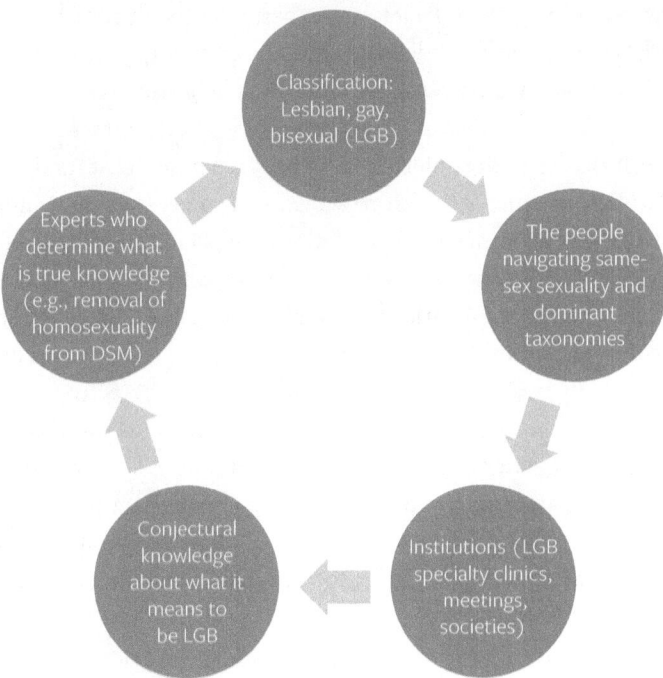

Figure 3.2 A looping effect associated with dominant taxonomies

This brings us back at last to our primary focus in this book: emerging sexual identities. In the same way that the looping effect has helped to create and shape dominant frameworks of LGBTQ+ identities, we see a similar looping effect occurring in the creation and evolution of emerging sexual identities. Let's consider how this looping effect might be at work by exploring young people's experience (especially in social and digital media) as they curate and perform their emerging sexual identities.

The Looping Effect and Emerging Sexual Identities

To be clear, when we say that the looping effect has shaped emerging sexual identities, we are not suggesting that society has created new sexualities per se. That is, the experiences that lead to labeling with emerging sexual identities are not completely invented by society. Nor was homosexuality. Nor was heterosexuality.

Hacking, in his discussion of the looping effect, frames looping in relation to a philosophical debate between nominalists and realists. Nominalists argue that new distinctions create new realities that "effectively came into being" alongside their nomenclatures.[18] To one extent or another, nominalists hold that categories are established by humans rather than just existing in nature. Realists, in contrast, hold that such distinctions have always been real and were simply waiting to be named and classified correctly.

If you are a nominalist, you would be inclined to say that homosexuality, heterosexuality, gay, lesbian, and emergent sexual identities have been invented by society. If you are a realist, you would be inclined to say that these various distinctions have always been real and were just waiting for people to name them and correctly classify them.

Hacking argues for a middle ground, which we find appealing as well. He describes this middle ground as "dynamic nominalism," arguing that kinds of people were not so much *discovered by* science as they were *evolving alongside* science; that is, "a kind of person came into being at the same time as the kind itself was being invented."[19] Hacking observes the phenomenon of dynamic nominalism within many different categorical shifts. For example, in his discussion of autism and autistic people, he writes:

> Autism narratives are not just stories or histories, describing a given reality. They are creating the language in which to describe the experience of autism, and hence helping to forge the concepts in which to think autism.... They are developing ways to describe experience for which there is little pre-existing language.[20]

Hacking contends that autism narratives do not so much provide an "insider view" of autism as they provide language for describing experience. At the same time that stories are being told using the available language of the diagnosis, a "new discourse is being made up right now, i.e., ways of talking for which the autobiographies serve as working prototypes."[21]

In the case of emerging sexual identities, autobiographical accounts are being worked and reworked in real time on digital and social media platforms.[22] In the earlier case of "homosexuality," we've seen the significant role of science and diagnostic nosology as part of the looping effect. This emphasis on scientific expertise was an essential development in the formulation of what we are referring to as the dominant taxonomy, which tends to emphasize sexual orientation's unchosen nature. With emergent sexual taxonomies, by contrast, these identities are being cocreated, enacted, and performed primarily in digital and social media, as we will explore in greater detail below.

Hacking is concerned with categorization and entities generally rather than with specific questions about emerging sexual (or gender) identities. However, his insights into the looping effect are relevant here. As we turn to emerging sexual identities, neither nominalism nor realism alone can explain all the current trends. It is certainly fair to ask: Are emerging sexual identities preexisting realities that are only recently being recognized? Or are we discussing experiences of sexuality (e.g., graysexual, biromantic) that are coming into being while they are being practiced, rehearsed, and embodied? We believe that nonnormative sexualities have been experienced throughout history, which would seem to challenge the nominalist position. Yet we are not prepared to claim that emerging sexual identities are discrete ontological realities that have just been waiting to be discovered and classified, which would seem to challenge the realist position. Nonnormative, emerging sexual identities appear to have evolved alongside changes in society, shaped not only by institutions and experts but also by those individuals who are navigating same-sex sexuality and other experiences. This observation is very much in keeping with Hacking's idea of dynamic nominalism.

The current prevailing understanding of nonnormative sexuality has long been separated from the residual paradigm of diagnostic mental health nomenclature. It is now broadening even further—beyond the dominant typology of gay, lesbian, and bisexual—in favor of emerging categorizations. These emerging sexual identities did not arise due to changes sanctioned by experts; rather, they are being cocurated in digital and social media, where sexual identities are tried on, practiced, rehearsed, and revised.

As we apply the looping effect to emerging sexual identities, recall that a looping effect can be accounted for in five parts: (1) classification, (2) the people, (3) institutions, (4) knowledge, and (5) experts. We illustrate the five parts as they pertain to emerging sexual identities in figure 3.3. We begin with (1) classification, which includes many (varied) emerging sexual identities. These identity labels are curated and enacted largely in digital and social media by (2) the young people who experience nonnormative sexualities. In some cases (as for asexual people), their experiences don't seem to fit well within dominant forms of classification; in other cases, even though a dominant label like "gay" could accurately describe their experience, they prefer a more precise label. In either case, they continue to interact (as they have undoubtedly been interacting) with diverse, microminoritized identity labels. We can still discuss (3) institutions in terms of societies, meetings, and so on (e.g., The Trevor Project), although they appear to be less salient than they would have been in the shift from "homosexuality" to "gay, lesbian, bisexual," from residual to dominant. We agree with Rob Cover that digital and social media are the stages upon which linguistic constructs for emerging sexual identities are practiced and reworked into commonly accepted (4) knowledge that is shared and circulated in society.[23]

This modified looping effect appears to bypass the role of experts (see modified looping effect in fig. 3.3). The working and

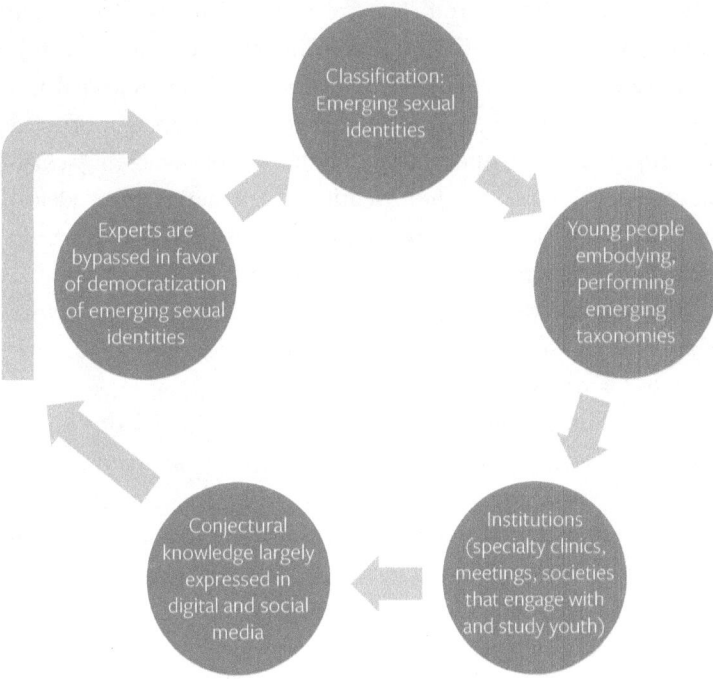

Figure 3.3 A modified looping effect associated with emerging sexual identities

reworking of emerging sexual identities is not contingent upon expert validation in the same way as previous understandings of dominant and residual identity taxonomies. Emerging sexual identities are created and curated within peer groups through digital and social media. They are performed in digital and social media. From these digital and social media emerge conjectural knowledge defining what we know about a topic. This suppositional knowledge includes a shared understanding of specific, emerging sexual identities and how that understanding is revised over time, and it gradually migrates into the broader cultural discourse of emerging sexual identities. This conjectural knowledge of emerging sexualities is created, performed, and embodied in (and increasingly reflected in) digital media and social networks.

In the realm of emerging sexual identities, we see conjectural knowledge in a study from The Trevor Project in which over one hundred sexual identities (and over one hundred gender identities) were used by participants.[24] We noted earlier that sexual and gender identities are often combined and form microminoritized identities; there are countless combinations across emerging sexual and gender identities for the formation of microminoritized identities (for example, when a teen states that they are a "biromantic demigirl"). When individuals' self-identifications are compiled into public knowledge through surveys like this one, they further shape the possibilities for emerging sexual identities and, ultimately, for young people's sense of self.

In the looping effect, the curation of this knowledge about sexuality has historically required (5) experts, who determine for society what counts as valid knowledge and offer guidance about how to respond, including how best to use specific (4) knowledge as a society. Ordinarily, as a body of knowledge increases, experts arise who weigh in on how we are to understand the phenomenon being classified.

With emerging sexual identities today, we're seeing the role of experts diminished. In their place, digital media is on the rise as a means of creating local expertise among those who embody emerging sexual identities. In other words, in the case of emerging sexual identities, experts are not centered as they were with the move from "homosexuality" to "lesbian, gay, and bisexual." Instead, experts are decentered or even bypassed in favor of the localized embodiment of emerging sexual identities.

In Hacking's discussion of how the looping effect relates to autism, he notes the important distinction between expert perspectives and other perspectives on autism in society. Douwe Draaisma further explores this distinction and its significance for society's understanding of autism:

> The very act of labelling initiates a complex interaction between the label and the perception and understanding of the person so labelled. Autism is no exception. Labels such as autism, Asperger syndrome or PDD-NOS [pervasive developmental disorder not otherwise specified] carry connotations and consequences, and these will influence pedagogical and educational practices. This interaction takes shape in a world in which psychiatry is not the only, perhaps not even the most important, force of influence. Today, the processes that shape the general understanding of Asperger syndrome and autism have come to be distributed over persons and institutions, literature and film, education and media. A better understanding of the autistic condition and the talents that may come with it demands that we should carefully observe the intricate interaction between the "expert" view of autism and the general perception of autism as it manifests itself in the way autistic persons are represented in novels, biographies, autobiographies and movies. That there is such a thing as a general perception of autism, perhaps best thought of as a *set* of stereotypes, is graphically brought out by what movies need or need not show to explain the autistic condition.[25]

In the case of autism, the expert view is contrasted with the "general perception" of autism in society—what Hacking calls "conjectural knowledge." This general perception by the public has been an important element of society's understanding of and experience with autism.

With emerging sexual identities, we see a diminished tendency to juxtapose the expert view with general perception. Rather, as we have suggested, expert views have been largely decentered and replaced by general perception and individual self-understanding. Note that the expert view (from psychiatry, psychology, and related mental health fields) was important in removing homosexuality from official diagnostic nosology; however, in the case of emergent sexual identities such as the ace spectrum, peer-group cocreation in digital and social media contexts exercises much more influence than experts in shaping classification and self-understanding.

In an interview we conducted about identity labels, one participant told us about their experience of the "asexual" label:

> One that really stuck out to me was Ace, like asexual. I was like, "Oh my gosh, I don't feel sexual," or "I don't feel romantic attraction at all." [Finding a label that fits] is awesome. I felt like that internally, but I did not want to say it out loud, because I wasn't sure people would be like, "Oh well, you're just too young." . . . [Age] 14 was the moment where I was like, "That's old enough." I used "gay" for myself as an umbrella term, but not like the literal gay. . . . Gender-wise, I also identify as gender non-conforming or GNC. . . . In middle school, I was getting dressed. I had braided my hair so it was out of my face . . . and I looked in the mirror . . . and I went, "*That's* not a girl." And it was very strong and very—it was inward—like in. It was a feeling, but it was more than a feeling . . . like it had vocabulary, and I was stunned cuz I had never felt like that, and I said, "Okay," and then I went to breakfast with my dad. . . . My day went on like normal, but internally I felt like, "Oh my gosh, I've never felt not like a girl before," and it was very exciting.[26]

It will be interesting to see whether the use of digital and social media as an avenue to authenticity and performance leads to further changes in conjectural knowledge or if such changes require some sanctioning by experts as to which designations are meaningful in society. Put differently, emerging sexual identities may be given a stamp of approval by experts after the fact, but it will not be experts who tell this population much of anything about what counts as knowledge about them. Where emerging sexual identities and microminoritized identities go from here is hard to predict.

What results from the looping effect of emerging sexual identities in our culture? One of the developments is the account of diverse sexual identities that are frequently contrasted to expressions of sexuality, orientation, and identity that have been derived, at least in part, from Judeo-Christian norms. The mainstream LGBTQ+ community certainly seems supportive of recognizing more expansive nonnormative sexualities and genders, which will be important when we turn our attention to ministry perspectives.

We caution our readers to be aware of the impact our rapidly changing culture may have on how people think about themselves, their sexual identity, and the options that lie before them. None of us may fully appreciate how cultural forces shape our categories of self-understanding.

Another important concept from Hacking—especially for Christians engaging the topic of sexual identities—is the idea that a classification can be ascribed by experts or by society at large but then rejected by the person being classified. He uses the example of "Hispanic," an ethnic kind created as a designation by the Bureau of the Census. This ethnic kind came into being as many people began to see and refer to themselves as Hispanic, affecting people individually and as a group in their understanding of themselves and their history. However, not everyone for whom the designation "Hispanic" was created has adopted it for themselves; some have rejected that label in favor of "Latino" or another designation.[27] The knower can ascribe a classification to the known, but the known can choose to adopt or reject that classification.

This principle has significant implications for our discussion of sexual identities. The mainstream gay community has historically adopted new language for themselves through the process of self-ascription, and younger sexual minorities are continuing to do so through the adoption of emerging sexual identities. Yet not everyone to whom this classification is applied will necessarily resonate with it personally. Some people who are classified as "gay" or another sexual identity label will reject that identity label in favor of other ways of thinking about themselves and their same-sex sexuality.

Concluding Thoughts

In Christian ministry and parenting, many people ask whether rejecting certain sexual identity labels should be encouraged as a matter of Christian obedience. If a person's experience is classified by experts or by broader society as "gay" or another sexual identity label, what role should that person play in accepting or rejecting the classification? The ex-gay movement, for example, has encouraged Christians to reject self-ascribed labels, and they discourage anyone entering their ministries from using the identity labels of "gay," "lesbian," "bisexual," or "queer." Other Christians who do not believe in the efficacy of sexual orientation change may still encourage same-sex-attracted people to reject self-ascribed labels like "gay." We'll discuss these two approaches to rejecting self-ascribed labels—sometimes called Side X and Side Y—and a range of other considerations and controversies in chapter 4.

Based on everything we've learned in the last three chapters about emerging sexual identities, what should Christians walking alongside someone with this experience do (in various roles as parents/ministers/etc.)? That's what we'll explore in part 2.

PART 2

IDENTIFYING A MINISTRY MODEL

CHAPTER 4

Controversies in Ministry

Jamal, a thirteen-year-old, sat in the back of the youth room, observing everything. The other kids were playing a game to kick off the night, but Jamal couldn't stop thinking about what he'd read the previous night. Jamal had been online researching same-sex attraction and faith, trying to figure out how he could have crushes on guys and still follow Jesus. During his research, he came across the work of a Christian organization that seemed to help people like him. As he scanned the website, he felt his panic increase. He read about how homosexuality is caused by early parental-attachment wounds and/or abuse in childhood. He thought back to his childhood, racking his brain for examples that fit the stories on the website. He thought to himself, "I don't remember ever being abused. Could it be that I was abused and blocked it out?" He felt enormous self-doubt and panic creep in. "I thought I had a good childhood, but maybe I'm wrong."

Jamal kept reading and searching for answers. He stumbled onto another website that seemed credible and was linked as a resource by a prominent Christian speaker who came to his Christian school last year. The website talked about how homosexuality is caused by a distant father. Jamal's dad, who was in the military, *was* gone a lot when Jamal was young. They were closer now, but Jamal could resonate with wishing his dad was around more. "Did my dad's job make me this way?" Jamal wondered angrily.

This began Jamal's search for the thing that made him attracted to men. It also began his increasing distance from his parents, especially his father, because he resented his absence and assumed it to be the cause of his sexual attractions. He spent so much time and energy on this search that he found it difficult to participate in youth nights, and after a few months of feeling disconnected from his youth group peers, he stopped going.

Jamal spent the next few years praying only when he was overthinking at night. He would beg God to "make it go away," and he became increasingly distraught when, despite his best efforts and prayers, this didn't happen. Despair set in more and more; he grew more isolated from others the longer his attractions remained.

Eventually, he stopped looking into faith-based resources altogether, feeling disconnected from God, his family, and his faith community. He sought out secular resources to understand his sexual orientation and was drawn to the term "androsexual" to talk about his sexual orientation. He looked back on his time searching for the cause of his sexuality as a time laden with shame and self-rejection.

The story of Jamal is not an isolated one. Christian young people have been offered resources of all kinds for addressing sexuality questions. These resources vary significantly, and it can be difficult for youth and their families to know what ministry approaches and resources will be helpful for them. Many Christian resources about sexuality use the residual taxonomy of "homosexuality" and simply avoid or reject more modern language, causing them to speak past many of the very people they are designed to minister to. These resources also tend not to engage robustly and critically with the emergent taxonomy of sexual orientation flowing from queer theory.

Ministry Gap Between Dominant/Emergent and Residual Taxonomies

We both have provided mental health training in Ukraine. When we first visited Ukraine, several years before the Russian invasion of the country, it was not uncommon on the eastern side of Ukraine to speak with Ukrainians who spoke both Ukrainian and Russian. Greetings in Russian were commonplace. If we were to visit today, a few years into the current war, we would have to be very careful not to use Russian when speaking to Ukrainians. Their experience of the language has been imbued with significance via the war. Ukrainians today hear Russian spoken by Americans in a very different way than they would have prior to the war. Carelessness on the part of American visitors to Ukraine could cost goodwill and relational capital. We have learned that it is important to be prudent in navigating those cross-cultural relationships given the sociopolitical climate.

Similarly, we believe that being prudent with language is important in ministry to sexual minority youth. Many Christians in counseling or ministry today draw upon a residual taxonomy for sexuality, and they're often unaware of the implications of this language for the people they're talking to. This unawareness about language is a bit like speaking Russian to a Ukrainian today. While sexual minority youth can understand the basic meaning of residual language like "homosexual," the language is often offensive and can potentially burn bridges you hoped to cross.

In addition to using residual language, many Christians in counseling and ministry to sexual minority youth are also influenced by the philosophical frameworks that gave birth to that language. When they think of "homosexuality" in their residual framework, their primary points of reference are concepts like sin and abnormality. They can be so conversant in their Christianized residual framework that they assume it is dominant. And yet, while their residual taxonomy may feel dominant for them and the people in their religious circles, most youth are raised in a broader social context where the taxonomy of "gay, lesbian, and bi" has become dominant. For these youth, even this dominant taxonomy has started to be replaced by emergent taxonomies, which we discussed extensively in part 1.

Youth are steeped in this social context and, if anything, deviate from the dominant taxonomy only by embodying and performing an emergent taxonomy of ever more expansive sexual and gender identities. They have few, if any, positive impressions of the residual taxonomies used in most churches today.

The ministry gap between residual and dominant/emergent taxonomies is already significant and hard to span. We predict that this span will only grow in the next decade. Soon, most Western youth will have spent their entire lives in a culture that assumes the possibility of gay marriage. Even today, most youth were too young to be paying attention to politics when the Supreme Court's 2015 *Obergefell v. Hodges* decision made same-sex marriage legal throughout the United States; as far as they're concerned, this has always been the case.

This difference between today's youth culture and most church cultures became obvious in a recent talk Julia gave to Christian youth. The number one question these youth asked had to do with Christian teachings on gay marriage and sexual morality. "What does God think about queer people?" they asked. "What does chastity look like if you are asexual?" another wondered. "Why does the church tell people they can't be queer when they are born that way?"

So many messages embedded in both dominant and emergent sexual taxonomies are taken for granted by young people today. Ideas of sexuality as *innate* and *immutable* or as *embodied* and *authentic* are pulsing through the veins of most youth today. It is the air they breathe; it is the water in which they swim. Yet most Christians we know are not particularly conversant in dominant and emergent sexual taxonomies. More to the point, they feel deeply concerned about how young people are influenced by those dominant and emergent taxonomies and the messaging embedded therein but struggle to identify any of the positive or neutral components of this language. They are trying to speak to youth from an exclusively residual taxonomy, and they respond fearfully to youth who do not already draw from a residual taxonomy. Further, they sometimes demand that youth simply abandon their language practices and adopt the adults' residual framework. It's as if they are speaking Russian to a Ukrainian and demanding the Ukrainian do the same: Some youth won't understand it, and some who understand will find it offensive and will disengage.

When we talk about offending youth, some readers may be tempted to respond, "Yes, and the gospel should be offensive," thinking of Mark 8:31–33 and 1 Corinthians 1:17–18. We agree that both the gospel and the cross are offensive by their very nature. However, we must take heed to not add elements to our ministry that go beyond the gospel, antagonizing youth more than necessary and compromising our ministry aims. We want to be aware of how language may burn bridges rather than build them, and we want to consider ways to have integrity around our convictions and engage linguistically in thoughtful and flexible ways.

We will undoubtedly see an increase in the number of sexual and gender identity labels available to youth. We will also continue to see combinations of sexual and gender identity labels that we referred to as microminoritized identities.[1] We predict that this future characterized by expansive sexual and gender identities will be a challenge for the church and for those in ministry. These emergent identities will likely lead to strong critical reactions from local church members, especially those who are invested in a broader culture war around sexuality and religion.

We believe that this ministry gap between generations and language preferences is the most significant obstacle to effective ministry to sexual minority youth today. Too often, we are seeing teens leave behind their faith as a result of their Christian community's lack of meaningful engagement with dominant and emergent sexual identities. Because they don't hear Christians addressing the language and experiences that they and their peers live in, they seem to increasingly leave behind the hope that life as a Christian is possible for them.

This chapter provides an overview of current Christian controversies in caring for sexual minority and otherwise sexually diverse youth. These include efforts to change orientation and debates about language, postures of ministry, and models of ministry. In light of our discussion in the first half of this book, we will acknowledge the challenges and limitations we face in our current ministry landscape. We'll conclude with what we believe constitutes a hopeful and sustainable vision in Christian ministry for sexual minority youth.

The Question of Change

We (Mark and Julia) both have been in ministry and counseling settings where some people promote sexual orientation change efforts (SOCE). In our experience, this promotion happens primarily in Christian ministry spaces, and it usually relies on a residual taxonomy that views homosexuality as a psychological illness needing to be healed through spiritual or psychological intervention. Some ministries that don't explicitly state a goal of sexual orientation change still hold out the value of change through spiritual or psychological interventions. In terms of ministry presence in the US, the peak influence of these ministries was probably in the 1990s, and their ministry approaches were closely tied to politics.

A few decades later, after the closing of Exodus International in 2013 and the increased cultural support for gay marriage culminating in the US Supreme Court's 2015 *Obergefell* ruling, how prevalent are orientation change ministries today? We've seen a somewhat diminished ex-gay presence among Christians who minister to or counsel sexual minorities. However, the question of change remains a current controversy, with some ministries still perpetuating claims that most people who try hard enough or have enough faith can expect to become straight through healing from childhood wounds.

A related claim is that Christians should work toward or pray for attraction change as a mark of their own sanctification. These expectations of attraction change have remained despite evidence that much of the reported change through ministry involvement may very well be behavioral (refraining from same-sex behavior) and identificational (no longer referring to oneself using "gay" as a sexual identity label) but not attractional in nature.[2]

Still Time to Care by Greg Johnson is the most comprehensive book to date examining the history of Christian ministry efforts to change a person's same-sex sexuality. Johnson's book highlights these ministries' focus on orientation change and their departure from historical evangelical understandings of sexuality. He also highlights the breakdown of these ministry approaches and their ripple effects into the present day. Honoring and critically reflecting on the residual taxonomy of an ex-gay script, he writes,

> The ex-gay script helped some people break with a past with which they no longer wished to associate, reinforcing their sense of being a new creation in Christ. It helped them center their life not on a narrative supplied by an unbelieving culture but on a narrative of change. But the ex-gay script left others unknown and therefore unloved, living behind a mask that hid the reality that their sexual orientation had not changed. It left them at the mercy of fellow believers who assumed it had changed or insisted that it would.[3]

The mental health community has experienced shifts in its understanding of efforts to change sexual orientation. Whereas there have historically been efforts to change orientation through therapeutic means, the field of mental health has moved away from such approaches due in large part to very limited research evidence showing attraction change is a realistic and frequent outcome.

Regardless of the effectiveness or ineffectiveness of orientation change efforts, the ex-gay framing of "homosexuality," following a residual taxonomy, tends to be lost on youth who are primarily operating from an emergent taxonomy. This doesn't mean merely that the strength and direction of attraction are fixed, per se. In fact, there has been greater recognition in recent years of the potential for sexual fluidity among sexual minorities, particularly sexual minority women.[4] This research finding has challenged the previously prevailing understanding that sexual orientation is always and permanently fixed; rather, we may see some fluidity for some people.

Some readers may wonder if, in the emergent categorizations, sexual identity is based on attraction or behavior. What we see most often today is identity labeling framed around one's experience of attraction (or lack thereof) rather than one's relationship status or sexual behaviors. Many teens who adopt emerging sexual identities will share they have not been in any romantic relationships or engaged in any sexual activity. Whereas residual categories (e.g., "homosexual") reference behavior as a gauge of identification, and dominant categories ("gay," "lesbian") allow for some latitude in this regard but seem to account for at least attraction and sometimes behaviors, emergent categories reference an experience of attraction.

In any case, the question of whether counseling or religious ministry participation can lead to a change of orientation remains quite controversial—and, as we've said, there is relatively little evidence of the efficacy of these efforts. Many states have passed legislation to stop SOCE among minors, and many young people have felt relieved by this move. Not only, then, is the ex-gay narrative operating from residual taxonomies that will be far removed from the frameworks of the young people we seek to minister to, but it is also seen as a threat to people from a legal perspective, further disparaging the credibility of those who would be operating with that lens.

While there may not be as many outward-facing ministries attempting to change sexual orientation as there once were, the messages that flow from change ministries persist in our Christian circles. Sometimes, the pathway of attraction change is presented as a realistic option in charismatic healing or deliverance ministry circles. How often have you heard that if a gay person could only heal early childhood wounds, they would be able to be "delivered from homosexuality"? Or the encouragement from religious leaders for a gay man or woman to "try dating someone of the opposite sex, because you never know"? This kind of counsel has led to enormous disappointment for many clients we've met with, who have attempted to change their orientation to no avail. We are increasingly aware that reliance on orientation change narratives will lead to a discrediting of Christian ministry approaches more broadly.

Although the framework of homosexuality as a psychological illness is now residual, we continue to see some young people who disclose their sexuality wonder about the possibility of sexual attraction change. More often, we meet with Christian parents, religious leaders, and adult mentors who wonder about sexual attraction or orientation change for young people in their lives. Increasingly, we see youth being fairly comfortable with their experience of sexuality and thus being drawn to emergent taxonomies of sexual orientation and identity.

It is still important in counseling and ministry to understand the degree to which a young person desires to experience attraction change. This is no longer a common desire among young people, but it can still occur. As we saw with Jamal at the beginning of this chapter, an interest in attraction change may come from other stakeholders in a teen's life, including faith-based resources they have read that have offered this as a realistic hope. Keep in mind, too, that the desire to be straight can be a way sexual minorities

FOR PARENTS: STAY PRESENT AND INVITE CONVERSATIONS

We do not recommend that parents attempt to change their teen's attraction pattern or orientation. When teens find themselves with attractions, we recommend instead helping the teen bring these experiences into conversation with trusted adults, including parents, mentors, and a therapist. As parents, you can:

1. Receive your teen's story with a willingness to express love without that love hinging on attraction change. Parents can model this by saying, "I love you. The direction of your attractions does nothing to detract my love for you. The same is true for God's love for you. Whether your attractions persist or evolve over time, I am not going anywhere, and there are ways to glorify God as you learn to steward your attractions."

2. Acknowledge fluidity: A person's experience of attraction, labeling, and sexual behaviors can shift over the course of their life. You can acknowledge this without implying you believe your child's attraction or identification is a phase. Though natural fluidity will happen, it doesn't seem to be caused by a single variable or type of intervention.

3. Accept the current reality: Teens may be more comfortable than parents are with this. For parents, it is important to recognize the reality of their teen's current experience of attractions while recognizing that identity development occurs over years, not months. Parents may also need space to process their emotions about this so that they don't come out sideways (indirectly, through behaviors or actions).

4. Encourage a relationship with God: Teens can be encouraged to bring their experiences, emotions, and attractions before God in prayer, perhaps coming to a better understanding of his love for them in the midst of these experiences. They can build a trusting relationship with God where they would be willing to bring their experiences of attraction under God's sovereignty and guidance. Teens will benefit from being reminded that God's not surprised or scandalized by their experience but is ready to help them live virtuously in the midst of this, no matter how their orientation manifests over time.

respond to their shame, holding out hope to remain within the norms supported by their family and faith community.

When ministry leaders approach us in search of an avenue toward orientation change, we try to first demonstrate curiosity about what they are hoping for and how they came to see this as an ideal outcome for ministry. Our response has two parts: First, we ask what they mean when they ask about the possibility of change; second, we ask how they came to the conclusion that such steps would be the best way to respond to sexual attractions. We want to honor how the idea of orientation change functions for many Christians as a way of establishing or maintaining hope in an outcome that allows a person to serve God with their life as fully as possible. Locating hope is an important part of any kind of Christian ministry, but we gently challenge people against the notion that hope could be found only if these attractions would go away. In this case, while we do not direct people to pursue orientation change, we want to achieve insight into the request for this change and the desire for hope that is embedded in the request itself. We also offer that youth can find discernment regarding sexual behavior and identification regardless of the direction of their attractions, highlighting that hope is rooted in growing in Christlikeness, not attraction change.

Another question that comes up in Christian ministry or therapy connected to sexuality is whether meeting with a Christian minister or provider will amount to an attempt to change their sexual orientation, as Levi's story demonstrates. Levi asked to speak with us by phone about a month before his family consultation. He wanted to know whether meeting with a Christian therapist would amount to an attempt on our part to change his sexual orientation. He had heard from friends that a Christian counselor would push "becoming straight" on him and that he would be better off just canceling the appointment his parents had made.

Whereas the previous question (expressing a *desire* for orientation change) is far more common among parents and ministers, a question such as Levi's is more often asked by youth. For some youth today, their strongest association with Christian ministry or Christian mental health is sexual orientation change efforts. We have often explained that our approach to care is not to attempt to change sexual orientation. We do not measure attraction shifts as a goal or outcome of therapy and do not recommend that other therapists or ministries do this. Rather, we focus on personal congruence: helping a person live and foster their life in keeping with their beliefs and values.

How might we apply this principle in a nontherapeutic ministry context? We want to find a path forward that offers insight and wisdom for Christian believers without relying only on residual taxonomies and assumptions about sexuality. We believe Christian insight can and should be communicated in ways that speak to the dominant and emergent sexual taxonomies preferred by the broader culture and especially by young people today.[5]

The work of these next few chapters is to develop a Christian framework that can pierce through the emergent taxonomies young people are drawing from. Moving away from sexual orientation change means moving toward sexual stewardship in the realm of sexuality, as we will discuss more in chapter 6. Moving away from orientation change also means humbly acknowledging that opposite-sex attraction, too, can be distorted by lust. When we think about how heterosexuality has sometimes been put forth as a ministry goal, we are reminded that the majority of our Western society is heterosexual, and heterosexually attracted people do not have the market cornered on sexual morality or health. Too often a ministry approach that focuses exclusively on orientation change and sets as a goal subsequent heterosexual marriage asks far more from sexual minorities than Christ has asked of them.[6]

The Debate About Language

The question of how young people who experience same-sex attraction should refer to themselves remains a controversy in Christian circles. This is probably one of the best examples of how conservative Christians have distanced themselves from dominant taxonomies of sexual identity—lesbian, gay, and bisexual—let alone the emergent taxonomies we discussed in chapter 1 (including graysexual, queer adjacent, biromantic, cupiosexual, fluid, gynesexual, and pomosexual). In our experience, Christians tend to be much more comfortable with the residual taxonomy of "homosexual" and the implication of either vice or psychiatric abnormality, or they demonstrate a preference for sticking with descriptive accounts of same-sex attractions ("I am a twenty-four-year-old woman who has experienced same-sex attraction since age twelve"). This gap in ministry language based on preferred taxonomies will continue to present a challenge in ministry circles.

We are not saying that language is unimportant in ministry. Not at all. But we are saying that if the bulk of your ministry strategy is to correct what you deem to be improper language, you are limiting your ministry's effectiveness in reaching a group of people operating from dominant and/or emergent taxonomies.

We have witnessed the stories of many young people who have shared that, upon disclosing to a person in ministry their sexual attractions, they were pretty quickly told the words they ought to use and avoid. As you can imagine, it was difficult for these young people to feel truly heard and understood when the first response to their vulnerable sharing was a person telling them what they ought to do and not do about it—including what words they were permitted to use to describe their experience. Many of us can likely relate to this.

When language is the focus of Christian ministries, as is the case with ministries that prescribe language to participants and filter out anyone who uses mainstream language, these ministries may miss an opportunity to reach a majority of sexual minorities. Prescribed language can leave a young person much less inclined to share other vulnerable information, closing the door on future engagement. It can lead to duplicity, where a young person feels they must use their listener's preferred language, even if that language feels alien to their own experience. They may code switch by using language that makes sense to them when they are alone or with their friends but then use ministry-approved language while at church or youth group. This division of language teaches young people to disconnect their internal life from their external religious life rather than creating room for them to consider what guidance God and the church have to offer in the realm of their sexuality over time.

The most contentious terminology within our communities appears to be the phrase "gay Christian," as well as forms of the phrase that convey commitment to Christian sexual ethics, such as "celibate gay Christian." Any of the emerging sexual identity labels would also likely be unsatisfactory from this perspective, if the rejection of dominant labels is any indication.

FOR PARENTS: ACKNOWLEDGE AND BE CURIOUS ABOUT TERMS

Parents can unintentionally signal that a young person needs to filter their language in the home. To avoid doing this, instead acknowledge to your teen that you are aware that teens use a range of terms to talk about sexuality these days. You may give some examples and then ask your teen, "What have you heard about this?" Or "What questions do you have about this?" This approach can facilitate conversation about language without the teen feeling as if you are too fragile to hear their perspective or will be shocked by what you have heard. You can also talk with your teen about the benefits and drawbacks of labels as they have evolved over time.

This controversy has come to a head in recent years, in part because of the increased visibility of "Side B gay Christians." What is a Side B gay Christian? This language can be traced back to a now-defunct ministry called Bridges Across the Divide. In an effort to promote good-faith dialogue, this organization chose to use the letters A and B to designate theological positions that do or don't affirm same-sex marriage for Christians rather than using more weighted language like "pro-gay" or "anti-gay." Over the years, additional letters have been added to the original A-B

Table 4.1
What the "Sides" Mean Today in the Christian Dialogue Among Sexual Minorities

Side A	A Side A gay Christian believes that same-sex behavior can be morally permissible in certain relationships, such as the commitment between two spouses of the same sex in marriage. This "side" tends to identify with many aspects of the mainstream LGBTQ+ community as a culture.
Side B	A Side B gay Christian views same-sex behavior as morally impermissible. These Christians may pursue celibacy or be in a mixed-orientation marriage in which one spouse is gay and the other is straight. They tend to identify to varying degrees with cultural elements of the mainstream LGBTQ+ community.
Side C	The Side C person is unsure or confused as to whether same-sex behavior is morally permissible. They might be actively seeking answers to that question, or they may have set that question aside for the time being and anticipate that they will get back to it when they have the energy to do so.
Side X	According to the Side X perspective, not only is same-sex behavior morally impermissible, but same-sex attraction and orientation are also sinful. Because of this, Side X Christians believe they should change their sexual orientation as a reflection of their own sanctification. They do not identify as "gay" and tend to use descriptive language (e.g., "same-sex attraction"). They also do not identify with any elements of the mainstream LGBTQ+ community.
Side Y	The Side Y person is not as confident as a Side X person that sexual orientation can change, but they share similar concerns about the inherent sinfulness of same-sex orientation and attraction. Like Side X, they do not identify as "gay," tend to use descriptive language (e.g., "same-sex attraction"), and do not identify with any elements of the mainstream LGBTQ+ community.

binary, mostly by expanding the nonaffirming Side B into three different "sides" (see table 4.1).

The increased visibility of Side B gay Christians has brought the discussion of labels to the forefront. This discussion has both pastoral and ministry elements. Some Christians view the use of these labels as identifying with sin and might offer arguments like the following:

> If you are gay, you are saying you experience same-sex attraction, which is at the very least a temptation to sin, perhaps even a sin in itself. Using the term "gay" before "Christian" establishes your identity in sin, which is harmful for you and harmful for others to see as a model. We don't allow others to identify with their sins, such as the "lustful Christian" or the "prideful Christian" or the "thieving Christian" or the "murderous Christian."

Of course, these statements do not go over well in the Side B gay Christian community. Their response is along these lines:

> We are using the language that is the vernacular for explaining sexual attraction or orientation today. We center our identity in Christ, and this is an important aspect of our experience. Descriptive language like "same-sex attracted" has been used by Side X and implies that the only Christlike path for us is to become straight, which is not a likely change, if it occurs at all. Younger people would not know of someone a few years older than them who is gay and following Jesus if we were not using "gay" to account for our experiences in a more public way. We are uniquely positioned for ministry to the mainstream LGBTQ+ community, and not using the vernacular will be a nonstarter for ministry. Many people talk about aspects of their experience as identifiers without meaning by the label that it is comprehensive or core to their sense of self.

You get the idea. This conversation is at an impasse. Rather than weighing in on one side of the impasse, we want to add another perspective: We see the rejection of identity language by some conservative Christians as criticism without an audience. By this we mean that their critique is rooted in residual taxonomies of sexuality, but it is directed toward Christians who use dominant (and presumably emergent) taxonomies. We raise this consideration to help you prepare yourself for ministry to a population that resides in the crosshairs of this debate.

Further, we want to highlight that a person can privately identify one way and publicly identify another. For instance, a man may privately see himself as gay, but being married heterosexually would lead him to be publicly identified as heterosexual. This is not problematic in and of itself, but if the public identification is done to accommodate others, the person may internally believe that "people can't handle me fully." The voice of shame is not far away, which says, "If you knew this aspect of me, you would reject me."

In ministry, we want to think about pathways that allow a person to approach God and others honestly, openly, and in the messiness of their lived experience. Fixating on language at the expense of building relationship limits the pathways and is ultimately obstructive.

Postures for Ministry Debate

A related controversy has to do with the postures for ministry debate. Christians have operated from various postures[7] in their ministry approaches.

The first approach is that of a *culture warrior*. The operating strategy of the culture warrior tends to involve lecture and cognitive disputation. We could think of this approach as being rooted both in a desire to uphold the truth and in a fearful "us versus them" mentality. In the case of emerging sexual identities, the culture warrior focuses the majority of their energy on refuting and discrediting queer theory, failing to look at its compelling elements, and generally framing people drawn to that theory as threats to be fought against. While feelings of fear and concern are certainly understandable in the current sociopolitical climate, as is protectiveness against theories that communicate a false understanding of the human person, we will be rendered much less effective when fears drive our ministry approach.

In our clinical and ministry experience, the two of us have witnessed this approach result in alienation for youth who may not be convinced by argument alone. Youth are often more focused on relationships than on arguments, which makes this strategy miss many of them. It can also lead to youth dismissing Christians as people who simply want to villainize "the other side" and "win the war." One Christian parent who used to cognitively dispute their queer-identifying loved one shared with us, "We won the battle, lost the war, and lost the relationship for years." The culture warrior approach can reinforce caricatures of Christians as "out of touch," "hateful," and "defensive."

The second approach we've observed is that of the *cultural capitulator*. The cultural capitulator's strategy can best be described as silence and/or apathy. We see this approach in ministry contexts where the significance of spiritual life and moral life is ignored or downplayed out of (understandable) fear of offending others or being thought of as "hateful." This approach can also flow from a lack of adequate formation in the principles of faith. In the context of emerging sexual identities, we see this approach as one where Christian beliefs about human sexuality are downplayed or outright rejected as "outdated," "bigoted," and "restrictive."

The outcome of this second approach can be a loss of distinction between Christian morality and cultural narratives about the nature of the person. Such capitulation can muddy the waters or even lead teens to reject Christian beliefs they were never fully given the opportunity to understand. It can treat moral relativism as the truest form of "love," although in reality apathy is deeply unloving. If Christian approaches to life look just like secular approaches, what would prompt a youth to orient their life around faith, which inevitably involves sacrifice and self-denial in many realms, including in the realm of sexuality?

A third approach, which we want to offer as a posture and framework for Christian ministry, is that of the *cultural ambassador*.[8] In this approach, the strategy is formation of self and others in Christlikeness. This approach is rooted in the courage to hold convictions, demonstrate compassion, and relate with civility. The outcomes we have seen from this ministry approach include clarity about the Christian position on sexuality, including engaging critically with queer theory. This clarity demonstrates that our beliefs are not fragile. Springing from these beliefs, we can engage with compassion and flexibility both toward students who are compelled by a Christian vision for life and toward students who have questions or reject this vision outright. This approach also allows for critical engagement with culture, where we can honor any and all points of alignment and common ground with culture while also helping youth consider points of disagreement and cause for concern in narratives offered elsewhere. When it comes to emerging sexual identities, we believe this approach could help form a generation of youth who engage critically with queer theory (among many other things), including both the aspects of queer theory that resonate with Christian faith and the aspects of queer theory that are at odds with a scriptural understanding of sex, gender, and humanity. We can speak to and account for emerging and dominant taxonomies without aligning with them outright. We can take a posture of curiosity about the appeal of emerging sexual identities and how they function for young people, opening up a more constructive conversation and reflecting on them in light of Christian considerations.

To form those around us in cultural ambassadorship, we must also be formed as ambassadors. This formation requires moving beyond either complaining about emergent taxonomies or uncritically adopting them.

Our formation as cultural ambassadors is not something we can conjure up through knowledge or encounters with people alone. It requires humility, prayer, solid formation in a range of Christian principles and teachings, and a willingness to suffer and be courageous for the sake of the good (2 Tim. 1:7). At the same time, this formation demands relational ministry that prioritizes care for real people in the trenches, including those who may be drawn into aspects of culture that concern us. We must be willing to give testimony to what we believe and why we believe it, without pitting truth against mercy and love. We want to model ourselves

> **FOR PARENTS: BECOME A CULTURAL AMBASSADOR**
>
> The postures described here can also come up in parenting approaches to sexuality. The *culture warrior* posture might default to lecture mode in parenting. Parents lecture when they feel the need to teach something, perhaps out of fear that the teen will not receive such information elsewhere. The challenge here is that we've all witnessed teens "glaze over" in these moments. They receive our input much better when we first get them talking about their perspective and when we assume that they have at least thought about the issue already. We might be surprised at the insights they offer when we give them space to develop their thoughts before sharing our own. The *cultural capitulator* parent might be hesitant to say anything at all, out of fear of saying the wrong thing. But being genuine and present with your young person is key, and without your guidance they will be left to their own devices. You can be honest that you are still learning and are afraid to misspeak but that you are also working to learn more about this terrain so as to be equipped to help. The *cultural ambassador* might engage with this process and use it as an opportunity to be formed in their own understanding of faith and sexuality. You can speak in Christlikeness and with gentleness, curiosity, clarity, and wisdom while also inviting dialogue and expecting resistance along the way as your teen wrestles with culture, sexuality, and faith.

after Christ himself, who spent enormous time on the margins; who came to call not the righteous but sinners; and who suffered, died, and rose from the dead that we all might know, love, and serve him (Luke 5:32).

Models of Ministry Debate

One last significant controversy among Christians who hold a historically Christian understanding of sexual ethics has to do with models of ministry. In the sexual identity ministry space, we see three models of care roughly aligned with the three "sides" that don't affirm same-sex marriage: some ministries focus on change of orientation (Side X), some on change of identity (Side Y), and some on change of behavior (Side B).[9] We discuss these models in terms of outcomes because the models are often known for what they say they can accomplish or what they value in terms of change. Let's discuss each model briefly before we offer our suggested model of ministry to accompany our ministry posture as cultural ambassadors.

Model 1: Change of Orientation (or Hope for Change)

As we discussed earlier in this chapter, change of orientation is perhaps the most well-known model of sexuality ministry for Christians. It reflects a Side X or ex-gay understanding in which the proper Christian goal is to help a person shift their orientation from homosexual to heterosexual. We see this model of ministry diminishing in many Christian circles; however, there are definitely areas in which this ministry model is still being practiced today.

Ministries that use this model may not always place an explicit emphasis on sexual orientation change. The framework may focus more on "healing from past wounds," with the implicit or explicit expectation that this process could lead to heterosexuality. These ministries may recommend resources, organizations, or therapists that believe that homosexuality has environmental causes and can be resolved when a person's unmet needs are resolved. We have heard of youth being drawn into these resources when they are recommended by credible Christian voices. Sometimes, the people who recommend these resources don't fully know the impact of such approaches.

Those who are drawn to this ministry approach have told us that to reject the possibility of change in orientation is to reject God's healing power. We certainly want to acknowledge that God can miraculously intervene in anyone's life in any way he chooses. People have reported "healings" and recovery from many kinds of unchosen experiences, and we believe this can happen for any aspect of human experience. At the same time, there is a difference between acknowledging the potentiality of a certain kind of change and holding out that change as a likely outcome and a measure of effective ministry.

People drawn to orientation change as a ministry approach often liken same-sex orientation to a kind of illness to be cured or a brokenness to be fixed. To speak into this view, we might use palliative care ministry as an analogy for sexual orientation ministry. Palliative care provides relief from pain or other symptoms of long-standing or besetting conditions, including terminal illnesses, but palliative care is not curative. We certainly acknowledge the possibility of radical and miraculous healing in cases of besetting conditions or even terminal conditions. It is also possible to pray for things like symptom reduction, and to experience symptom reduction, without a complete healing. This makes the question of "healing" more complicated than an on-off switch.

We would not recommend that churches only offer ministry approaches in which patients with life-threatening conditions are *expected* to pray for healing and expect to be healed. What are people to do and where are they to go when God doesn't heal, as is the case for many we love with life-threatening or terminal conditions? Is there a place for them if they are not praying for healing from something they did not choose and would love to be free from?

By way of imperfect analogy, we would ask the same questions of those drawn to a ministry approach that attempts to change orientation. Even if such change occurs in some cases, albeit rarely, is it prudent to offer this approach as a general rule or expectation for those experiencing same-sex sexual attraction? What are people to do and what recourse do they have when they find themselves with enduring sexual attraction that is nonheterosexual?

Efforts to change orientation are even more complicated to apply to emerging sexual identities. What does it mean for an aromantic-identifying person to experience sexual orientation change? What about a person who identifies as pansexual or queer? If the goal is simply orientation change, are we confident that heterosexual attraction is somehow less prone to lust than any other pattern of attraction?

We recommend that Christian ministers look into the resources currently offered and move away from those infused with the message that a person can and ought to want to experience a change of orientation to grow in Christlikeness. Again, we are not saying orientation change has never happened for individual people, but we are strongly cautioning ministry leaders against promising this when there is little evidence of the efficacy of this approach. Change of orientation puts a greater expectation on a person than historical Christian ethics have placed on Christian believers with enduring experiences of all kinds. Ultimately, in an ever-changing linguistic landscape, this ministry model will fail to connect to the actual questions of youth more than ever before.

One additional caution we have with this approach to ministry is that at times an influential person may have had their own personal experience of unique ways God worked in their life. We have seen a leader or youth speaker saying that God removed all attraction, orientation, or sexual temptation or that their old nature was characterized by these things and their new nature is free from them. They may hold out how God worked in their life as a standard for other people who are navigating sexual orientation and faith. We are not suggesting that God did not do what this individual claims he did in their life.[10] However, you may need to protect young people from standards imposed by others on the basis of one person's unique experience of God's work in their life. Making one unique experience the rule or expectation for all can lead to disillusionment.

Model 2: Change of Identity (or Freedom for Identity)

Some ministries may focus less on attraction change and more on relinquishing labels tied to mainstream gay narratives. These change-of-identity ministries can be rooted in what we previously called Side X or Side Y attitudes, but their focus is on helping people leave behind their sexual identity and form a new identity in Christ. Young people are encouraged to disidentify with the language and identity labels of the mainstream LGBTQ+ community.

Within the change-of-identity ministry approach, successful ministry means that a person might talk about themselves as "being delivered from homosexuality," "a former homosexual," or "a person struggling with same-sex attraction" whose "identity is in Christ."

People in these ministry settings have expressed that they prioritize identity change because they are concerned identifying with gay narratives can be a cause for scandal or misunderstanding. They have also argued that it is fruitless to "baptize" secular notions that are fundamentally at odds with a Christian worldview and that LGB language can prescribe an inevitable outcome of engaging in same-sex sexual behavior.

We find that these concerns, while often expressed by well-intentioned ministry leaders, fail to appreciate the nuances of language, categories, and the meanings imbued by these categories, which can vary from person to person. Given the looping effect, which we discussed at length in chapter 3, language use is not as simple as a person adopting or rejecting an identity—especially not for young people interacting with emerging sexual identities. They are engaging in a dynamic process that we fail to account for if we simply focus on the language they use when they walk in the door and try to change that language.

It is true that, as we have illustrated throughout this book, mainstream LGBTQ+ narratives are infused with theories at odds with a Christian worldview in their philosophical assumptions. At the same time, Christians throughout history have engaged with elements of broader cultural narratives, experiences, and traditions, "baptizing" these things with specifically Christian meanings and applications. We see people today attempting to uncover the aspects of mainstream LGBTQ+ culture that can be integrated into and submitted under their relationship with Christ. This integration can allow for powerful witness to the broader culture that the Christian doesn't always have to disidentify with every aspect of culture but can transform some aspects in distinctively Christian ways.

Certainly, there are multiple ways to transform culture. We would not imply that the only way for a sexual minority to transform culture is by using sexual identity labels. We know of sexual minorities who do not use identity labels for various reasons and who still share about their experience of sexual attraction as a testament to one of the facets that informs their experience of the world. However, we would also discourage ministries from discrediting the witness of Christian sexual minorities who use sexual identity labels.

We find that an approach anchored in changing identity gives too much power to language, as if language inevitably prescribes a particular way of being or determines the priority of certain identity labels as inevitably superior to a person's relationship with Christ. Further, we have found that people—especially youth—drawn to identity language will often simply assume Christian settings have no place for them if they are told they have to change identity labels to be part of the community. This is increasingly the case, as labels take on particular salience in younger generations.

Finally, we have seen many people who disidentified with sexual minority labels but continue to experience ongoing struggle with sexually acting out. We do not see any evidence that using identity labels makes one less able to live according to a traditional sexual ethic. Neither do we see evidence that avoiding these labels improves people's sexual stewardship. Spiritual growth, discipleship, and the cultivation of virtues can coexist with using language to communicate an aspect of experience that informs the particularities of that person's life of virtue.

Model 3: Change of Behavior (or Celibacy and Friendship)

Among Christians with a historically biblical understanding of marriage, ministry approaches that do not focus on orientation or identity tend to focus on behavior change and the pursuit of celibacy and friendship. This change-of-behavior approach does not look at orientation change as a likely outcome, nor is it particularly concerned with identity labels. Rather, the primary emphasis of these ministries is to help people who are pursuing celibacy or otherwise refraining from sexual behavior outside of Christian marriage. Some of these individuals might be in a mixed-orientation marriage in which they are married to a heterosexual spouse.

Broadly speaking, these ministry groups fit the definition of Side B we discussed above. At the same time, there is controversy around what Side B means in Christian contexts, so some ministries that might fit and function within the definition of Side B might not adopt the label. One goal of this approach would be to help participants reduce forms of sexual acting out that violate their Christian convictions, which may include hook-up encounters, same-sex sexual behavior in the context of a romantic relationship, viewing of pornography, or engagement in masturbation. Nevertheless, the focus of these ministries is not *merely* change of behavior.

These ministries are often focused more broadly on fostering growth in spiritual maturity. They often pursue this growth through spiritual disciplines that may previously have been made difficult by hurt in religious environments, including prayer, reading of Scripture, and communal practices such as corporate worship and church attendance. The goals of this approach go beyond "what a sexual minority is not engaging in" to "what a sexual minority *is* behaviorally engaging in" that promotes Christlikeness. It moves beyond a theology of "no same-sex sexual behavior" as the end of the conversation in ministry with sexual minorities. It moves young people toward a vision for their life that involves creating space for God to work in their circumstances and develop their gifts as they seek to live in accordance with Christian sexual ethics.

My (Julia's) dissertation explored the experience of loneliness and coping among Christian sexual minorities pursuing celibacy.[11] Most participants in this research still actively struggled with sexual acting out in some form and saw this as a moral concern to be repented of. Some participants went through periods of spiritual and practical challenges that led them to reconsider their pursuit of celibacy. Common reasons for their reconsideration included longings for a committed partner to experience life with, recognition of the daunting aspects of growing old in a society largely oriented around the nuclear family, meeting a person they were romantically drawn to, or feeling a lack of clarity about their theological convictions on sexuality. Doubts and reconsiderations like these are essential to consider in Side B ministry contexts, since people's value in these contexts may sometimes feel tied to their capacity to demonstrate (or at least feign) perfect conformity to Christian morality. Critics on all sides of this approach have attempted to undermine its validity by questioning the degree to which Side B people successfully practice sexual self-restraint in any given moment.

We believe that ministries addressing change of behavior are at their best when they move beyond behavioral compliance as an end in itself. C. S. Lewis points to this principle:

> We may indeed be sure that perfect chastity—like perfect charity—will not be attained by any merely human efforts. We must ask for God's help. Even when you have done so, it may seem to you for a long time that no help, or less help than you need, is being given. Never mind. After each failure, ask forgiveness, pick yourself up, and try again. Very often what God first helps us toward is not the virtue itself but just this power of always trying again. For however important chastity (or courage, or truthfulness, or any other virtue) may be, this process trains us in habits of the soul which are more important still. It cures our illusions about ourselves and teaches us to depend on God. We learn, on the one hand, that we cannot trust ourselves even in our best moments, and, on the other, that we need not despair even in our worst, for our failures are forgiven.[12]

The end that Lewis offers us, reflected throughout Scripture, is the process of spiritual growth, the cultivation of virtues, and development of habits of the soul. According to Lewis, the external visibility of this firm disposition is not as important as the interior journey we undergo in our ongoing conversion. This ongoing conversion, which each Christian is invited into, fosters dependence on God, humility, and recognition of our own ongoing need for God's mercy, grace, and presence.

Another insight from my (Julia's) dissertation is that some people found it helpful to view changes of behavior in the way they viewed the spiritual discipline of fasting. While others might criticize the "change in behavior" approach as one of repression or harmful self-negation, one interviewee shared that Scripture is replete with examples of God-honoring self-denial. She saw sexual abstinence as a way of not merely saying no to a good (or harmful) thing but saying yes to the space in her heart God would occupy by this no. The same could be said for fasting, where a person says no to the good of food (or a particular type of food) in a particular moment to create space for the nourishment that God is offering. This framework for ministry may be helpful, insofar as it does not assert that behavioral compliance (or fasting) is a way to earn God's love or reinforce self-loathing.[13]

One important nuance we recommend in change of behavior ministries is being careful not to frame God through a "prosperity gospel" lens, depicting God as rewarding virtuous people with a life of ease. Well-intentioned teaching of sexual stewardship, shaped by purity culture messaging, can sometimes imply that those who follow God in this area will be rewarded with everything they want in this life. When ongoing experiences of loneliness and disappointments in community arise, resentment and bitterness can fester toward God and others. This is fertile ground for ruptures in communal life, despair, and hopelessness for Side B Christians.

Some youth may be excited by the radical departure from mainstream narratives that they see in Side B pathways. However, these youth will need sustainable structures around them to cultivate ongoing spiritual practices and disciplines in discipleship. We would also do well to acknowledge that theological understandings of sexual ethics are not easy to translate cleanly into behavioral conformity; in other words, helping a young person arrive at historically Christian convictions about their sexual practices may be a very different process than helping them live in accordance with their convictions. Black-and-white thinking in ministry of this type can undermine the ultimate hope of ministry: growth in Christlikeness, which requires the recognition that growth in and of itself is a gift from God, not a reward for behavioral conformity.

In light of emergent sexual identities, we should also ask what "change of behavior" looks like for a person who identifies as "asexual" or with another label that involves a lack of sexual attraction. This question is a good example of how ministries that rely only on residual and dominant frameworks will be limited in their reach if they don't begin to account for the realm of emerging sexual identity labels.

What Is Our Hope for Sexual Minority Young People?

A question we often receive in talks is, What is the goal or hope for ministry to sexual minority youth? This is an important question. Our approach ought not to be aimless. Our faith is oriented around and undergirded by an assumption of a *telos*, an end or goal that orders our lives and relationships. To engage in ministry with the goal of "I'm happy if you're happy" would be to operate toward a relativistic end. Alternatively, to engage in ministry with the goal of "getting the right answers" would be to operate toward a purely intellectual end. Neither approach encourages young people to orient their lives toward the good, true, and beautiful.

As this chapter comes to a close, we want to return to the story of Jamal from the start of the chapter. Jamal, like some of the youth you will encounter in ministry, was initially plagued by scrutiny regarding what caused his same-sex attraction. He felt pressure to figure out the nature of his attraction prior to accessing his youth group environment. Eventually, he felt he had no choice but to walk away from his faith. He ultimately adopted an emerging sexual identity label rooted in a nonbinary understanding of gender.

Our hope for Jamal, as for all youth we walk with, would be that he could grow in Christlikeness through his time in youth ministry. We hope he could develop greater clarity about distinctively Christian beliefs and practices, discovering meaning and purpose in his life. At the same time, we want to acknowledge that youth like Jamal might not reach solid conclusions about all aspects of

Christian faith by the end of their time in youth ministry. If any one of us was expected to exhibit absolute cognitive assent to and absolute behavioral compliance with Christian morality (which we do well to remember goes beyond sexual morality), all of us would be unwelcome in our churches. We want to offer Jamal clarity about Christian teachings and the reasonable nature of our beliefs while also inviting him to bring his ongoing questions and doubts *to* God and Christian believers without fear.

We also want Jamal to have opportunities to experience love, joy, peace, and other gifts that flow from unity with God. We hope that Jamal's youth ministry lays a foundation of prayer, community, and other spiritual disciplines, guiding Jamal along a path where he grows in Christlikeness, in sanctification. Another way to word this is a path where Jamal's intellect, will, and behavior "gradually and resolutely approach Christian perfection."[14]

Another important hope in ministry is that we can help Jamal identify and remove obstacles that would prevent him from such growth. Each person we meet with in ministry has a different set of obstacles in their path of faith. Few young people walk a pristine path; our experience has been that the path for youth navigating emerging sexual identities is filled with obstacles and distractions. Common barriers for sexual minority youth include the belief that they are deficient because of their sexual attractions, are unworthy of being known by God and others, or are required to hide aspects of their experience to be part of the community. Other barriers may include the narratives of moral relativism or queer theory, which very often invite a rejection of absolute truth and a repudiation of sex and gender norms, including the very norms that uphold Christian marriage.

It is important to take a long-term view in ministry. In most cases, we will have the opportunity to walk with a teen for only a few years. This time span inherently limits what we can expect to bear witness to. Adolescence is a time of great change, exploration, and detours along the route. For many youth, we will witness them wrestling in this season much more than we witness them landing solidly in all aspects of their faith. At the same time, there are models of youth living vibrantly for God throughout history, and we don't want to assume our youth can't step confidently into a life of faith.

We do well to acknowledge and remind ourselves that perfection in any season of life is not the goal, even while we seek to "be perfect . . . as your heavenly Father is perfect" (Matt. 5:48). God delights in us, as nonlinear as our path toward him may be. In ministry with youth, especially in the current landscape, we will benefit from surrendering the youth we love to God's sovereignty, offering our own lives to them as models of what it looks like to imperfectly pursue God above all else.

Concluding Thoughts

In this chapter, we introduced you to several controversies in ministry circles today. These included the ministry gap between dominant/emergent and residual taxonomies, the change debate, the debate about language, the debate about postures for ministry, and the models of ministry debate. Our desire was to present each of these controversies, speak into them to some degree, and move us toward a model of ministry that answers the question, What is the goal or hope for ministry to sexual minority youth? From a ministry perspective, we shared how we want young people to have a *telos*, an end goal that orders their lives, that provides them with perspective and that gives them hope. We invite young people to access a spiritual life in Christ, a life in which they grow closer to him and know him more and more.

CHAPTER 5

A Relational-Narrative Approach to Ministry

"I always felt different as a little girl," Avila shared. "Other girls liked to play with Barbies and play makeup, but I didn't care about those things. I didn't quite know what to make of it when I was younger, but as I hit age ten or eleven, I started to notice other teen girls as attractive and didn't have the same experience with teen boys. Now, at the age of seventeen, even though I see other girls as attractive, I don't feel strong romantic desire for anyone. I guess I could at some point, but for now I use 'aromantic' to talk about my attractions. I haven't told anyone in the youth group, and only one of my siblings knows, because I think I'd lose friends over this. I don't think my parents would kick me out of the house, but some days I do worry about what they would think of me if they knew. I feel like I really don't fit in anywhere, kind of like how I felt as a kid. I want to be connected to God and my church, but I hear how they talk about people like me. It just feels too risky to let people in. What I think about my identity is a whole other thing. I use labels, but sometimes I feel conflicted when I talk about it with my queer friends, because they don't get my tension with my faith. I just joined my youth group, so I really hope I can begin to share about my sexuality and not have to filter too much."

This chapter lays a foundation for ministry and counseling approaches with youth like Avila, anchored in our understanding of how sexual orientation develops for sexual minority youth. The aim (or *telos*), as we stated in chapter 4, is to orient youth in Christlikeness. In addition to knowing where we hope to go with youth, we also need to know where they are coming from as they step into our faith communities. In this chapter, we will examine the arc of a young person's journey leading up to and through their time in our churches.

We recommend a narrative approach to sexual identity development that encompasses many potential "storylines" for sexual identity. That is, we want to account for the diverse experiences of youth by identifying some common experiences as "chapters" that can be assembled into a larger story. In our previous research, we've asked sexual minority Christians to share about their sexual identity development and faith by identifying and naming key chapters in their story. When it comes to understanding youth, then, we want to understand what kinds of chapters are most often part of their stories. In the story of Avila, for example, her earliest chapters were about childhood and gender atypicality, followed by first experiences of sexual attraction and possible sexual behavior. Then came disclosure to others, followed by a more synthesized sexual identity and sense of community.

By recognizing the common chapters shared by Avila and other young people with similar stories, we can better anticipate their current needs and what it might look like for them to direct the rest of their story toward growth in Christlikeness. Christian ministers often ask us, "What is life like for a Christian youth navigating sexual identity questions in our faith communities?" This chapter will help you answer foundational aspects of that question.

A Narrative Understanding of Sexual Identity

To get at the common chapters in the lives of sexual minority youth, we find narrative therapy's contributions to be incredibly helpful. A narrative approach considers a person's life as a story, and we recommend a person come to reflect on the chapters of their own story, especially as it relates to sexual identity development.[1]

When we think about narrative in counseling and ministry, we want to first consider that the broader culture influences individuals to see themselves a certain way. The ways of seeing themselves can be understood as unhelpful stories people tell themselves about their experiences. These ways of seeing (or construals) lead to problem-saturated stories, which leave people powerless and contribute to their relating to others in keeping with the problem stories that have been spoken over them and internalized.

> Not only do we, as humans, give meaning to our experiences by "storying" our lives, we are empowered to "perform" our stories through our knowledge of them. . . . Some of these stories promote competence and wellness. Others serve to constrain, trivialize, disqualify, or otherwise pathologize ourselves, others, and our relationships.[2]

The stories we perform that tend to constrain us could be thought of as problem narratives. Those stories that promote competence and wellness could be thought of as counternarratives.

Problem Stories of Sexual Minority Youth

We see youth trying to answer questions they are already naturally asking as they internalize the problem stories offered to them. Two primary questions we see all young people asking frequently, especially sexual minority youth, are "Am I normal?" and "Am I wanted here?" These two questions are important for those in ministry (and counseling) to be familiar with and prepared to respond to. From the narrative perspective, our answers to those two questions can be a part of a counternarrative that helps young people understand who they are (identity) and what community they are a part of (community). Whatever counternarrative we offer to the default narratives young people have received should answer the questions "Am I normal?" and "Am I wanted here?"

Think about what a young person growing up in the church might hear about gay people or the gay community that would inform how they might answer those two questions. (We will use the dominant taxonomy of "gay" here, since most churches have not yet engaged with emerging sexual identities.) In many churches, young people encounter what we call a dominant narrative of *abomination*. They hear Christians say gay people are "going to hell" and are "abominations."

Let's set aside theological arguments about salvation for a moment and just look at how this language functions as a dominant narrative or a problem story that a young person internalizes.[3] They know that they experience same-sex attractions, as do members of the mainstream gay community. When churches say that "to be gay is to be an abomination," some youth internalize that *they* must be an abomination. When they hear and internalize this message, it becomes a problem story or dominant narrative that makes it difficult for them to imagine a future where they are a follower of Christ who experiences same-sex attraction. The way they are inclined to answer the two questions we posed earlier is: "I am not normal, and I am not wanted here."

At the same time young people are making meaning from problem narratives in Christian communities, they are also encountering and internalizing other problem narratives from the mainstream LGBTQ+ community. The overarching problem narrative from the mainstream LGBTQ+ community could be thought of as one of *celebration*. This may include stories about being "born that way" and having an innate sexual orientation that is immutable. This could likely also include stories of assimilation into the mainstream LGBTQ+ community and affirmation of same-sex sexual expression. This problem narrative can also be a source of conflict for some young people, especially those who are Christians. They would answer the questions "Am I normal?" and "Am I wanted here?" with the sense that "I am normal and am wanted in the mainstream LGBTQ+ community, where I will be celebrated." Conversely, a young person might think, "I'm not wanted in the church, where they think I'm not normal, even though I wish I could find a place in a faith community."

In the midst of well-intentioned efforts to challenge errors within the mainstream LGBTQ+ problem stories, many Christians in ministry and counseling have underappreciated how emotionally satisfying and compelling these dominant stories can be (even if they are incorrect). Many Christian youth do not know how to navigate these ways of understanding themselves, these stories of celebration, in part because such stories are rooted in assumptions that do not line up with the values young people have been taught in the church.

Counternarratives That Honor Faith and Sexuality

In order to move beyond the above problem narratives, young people need a counternarrative. They need to learn new ways of seeing themselves, construing their experiences in more helpful ways that create space for them to belong and remain connected in their communities. We believe that Christian ministries can be good places for young people to learn and live into these counternarratives.

Young people need a counternarrative that answers the problem narratives of both *abomination* and *celebration* as they seek to answer questions about where they belong and if they are wanted.[4] They need help through counseling and ministry to construe their experience in more helpful ways, ways consistent with their faith and with the reality of their same-sex sexuality. You will remember that we commented briefly in chapter 4 on the fact that we help clients find congruence between their beliefs and their sexuality. The congruence a person experiences is a reflection of the emerging counternarrative, meaning a way of living out their faith and sexuality that challenges unhelpful narratives, whether those narratives be celebratory approaches from mainstream culture or shaming approaches within the church.

Much of ministry and counseling is holding out what has been declared "true" about a young person and challenging aspects of that narrative that are unhelpful and problematic. It would help to put yourself in a young person's shoes (if this isn't your own story) and to imagine what it would have been like to experience same-sex attraction in your local church and youth group. What might they have heard? What has been said? If nothing has been shared explicitly, how might they interpret silence on a topic? Use this thought exercise to evaluate both messages from your faith community and messages from the broader culture and LGBTQ+ community.

We are not recommending that when you hear a mainstream narrative embodied by a young person, you lead with strident disagreement. For example, we do not simply declare, "You are not to celebrate your same-sex sexuality!" as that type of pronouncement is seldom helpful for walking alongside developing youth. Further, we are not merely offering an immediate yes or no to young people's two burning questions. Rather, we begin by first understanding what they have heard. Then we ask about how they experience what they heard. If the mainstream LGBTQ+ narrative is compelling to them—and we think it would be to 99 percent of young people we know—we want to ask what is compelling about these stories as well as understand what they've heard so far from their faith community. Accounting for the dominant (or problem-saturated) stories of an adolescent navigating sexuality and faith takes time. We want to account for the way shame impacts their journey. Then we want to move toward building a counternarrative, with the constant invitation to allow that counternarrative to be shaped and infused with the light, truth, and life of Christ.

How Are Stories Related to Shame?

Sixteen-year-old Carlos couldn't make eye contact as he sat down to talk with his youth pastor, Patrick, at a youth prayer and worship night. Patrick had known Carlos and his family since they began attending the church eleven years ago. Carlos had been waiting for several years to share this secret with Patrick. At age eleven, Carlos noticed he had crushes on boys in his class as well as girls. He didn't expect this at all, and it shocked him. He had always dreamed of being a husband and father but figured no girl would want to marry someone "like him." Like many other young people navigating sexuality, he had talked to some online friends about his sexuality. He used the word "queer" to describe his attractions because his friends said that was the best word for people "figuring it out." He began to isolate more and more as time went

FOR PARENTS: BUFFER AGAINST UNHELPFUL NARRATIVES

Parents can proactively buffer against problem stories and shame as they parent preteens. Rather than exposing them prematurely to the vast terrain of emerging sexual identities at age eleven, you can begin by acknowledging that they will begin to notice crushes and attraction as they get older (if they haven't already). You can remind them that they can talk through these attractions with you, especially when they feel confused by attractions. You can acknowledge that sometimes teens experience crushes on people of the same sex, and that is something they can bring to you as well.

on, but he still felt connected to his youth group community and youth pastor. Now, five years later, he desperately wanted to tell his youth pastor about his sexuality, even though he was terrified. As he opened his mouth to share, he could feel this block. The shame was so powerful. No words came.

Shame is a deeply destructive emotional experience. It is different from the guilt we feel after having done something wrong. Rather, shame is the feeling that we are fundamentally flawed and that our flaws reflect most clearly who we are. Shame can be so debilitating that we hold others at arm's length, keeping them from knowing us because we assume that if they knew how flawed we really are, they would reject us just as we reject ourselves. Carlos's shame had kept him quiet about his sexuality for five years. He worried that Patrick, someone he really respected, would reinforce what he already believed about himself: "You are deficient, flawed."

Shame can result when we fail to meet standards based on social, cultural, and/or religious values and we attribute that failure to a deficit on our part. That attribution can be ours alone; it can also come from the social, cultural, and/or religious community of which we are a part. We can receive and internalize stories of who we are based on the values of our community. Those values can be conveyed through stories about people with shared characteristics, including attractions, orientation, or identity. In some communities, the stories people have been told about sexual minorities and the stories they tell themselves can result in shame. When stories like "Gays are an abomination!" are told by sources of authority in a young person's life, these stories quickly become canonical. From an attachment perspective, we can have attachment to institutions or communities, secure or insecure bonds to macrolevel attachment objects, like the church.[5] As with any attachment process, it is about how institutions or communities help members manage their fears, and for youth navigating emerging sexual identities (and other at-risk youth), who are always prone to fearful and insecure conditions, there is no secure base and safe haven for the development of healthy narratives. As a result, young people tell those stories to themselves over and over again, internalizing them. Internalized stories are hard to edit, and they are maintained by shame.

How do people respond in their shame? Most people who struggle with shame hide the source of their shame from others. We see this in Carlos's story above. Unfortunately, hiding makes shame worse. It reinforces the story of how others would reject a person if they just knew who that person *really* was. Many Christian sexual minorities like Carlos have chosen not to disclose their sexuality to others (that is, they elect not to come out) because they want others to think they are really "straight." They project an outward image that reflects their community's norms for sexuality, hoping this image will protect them in their social circles.

However, most sexual minorities who haven't disclosed their sexuality to others wrestle with a nagging question: "Would you still like me if you knew about my sexuality?" Others attempt to change their attractions so that they are straight. If they do not experience success in this endeavor, their shame will likely increase, especially if those in spiritual authority suggest to them that they have not tried hard enough to change or that they did not have enough faith in God to change. Still others may disclose their sexuality and have disastrous experiences that confirm to them the importance of staying in the closet. This, too, leads to an increase in shame.

How do we respond to shame in the context of Christian ministry? We will return to this important question in chapter 6.

Common Chapters in Storied Lives

The messages people hear, interpret, and internalize vary considerably. As we've already acknowledged, common narratives in this conversation range from abomination to celebration. The stories that are written in the lives of the people who internalize these messages vary considerably as well. The messages and possible storylines are told and processed at different developmental stages, impacting how different stories are heard, interpreted, and internalized.[6] As we discussed when we explored the looping effect, these youth are also interacting with a broader mental health community, church, peer groups, and media sources as they explore their identity.

Despite the wide variance in young people's stories, some chapters and themes appear to be common among most people navigating same-sex sexuality and faith. These include the preface to the story, making meaning out of same-sex sexuality, deciding whether to share the story with others, holding sexual identity and faith, and living the story itself (see fig. 5.1).

Preface to the story: gender atypicality in childhood. One of the most common experiences of sexual minority adults is feeling different from their childhood peers for gender-related reasons. When we say "gender-related reasons," we're referring to people's self-report that their "feeling different" had to do with their gender. For example, a boy might grow up feeling different from other boys if he shows interest in games or activities that are stereotypically associated with girls. Likewise, a girl can grow up feeling different from other girls if she perceives other girls as interested in activities that she has no interest in. Feeling different for gender-related

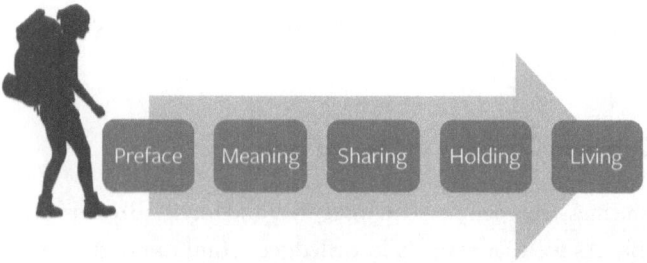

Figure 5.1 A narrative understanding of sexual identity

reasons is sometimes referred to as "gender atypicality." When LGBTQ+ adults are asked about their childhood, they frequently report that they felt different from other kids of their gender.

We saw this with Camila, who came for a consultation on both sexuality and gender. She reported that in her childhood, she was known as a tomboy. She was into playing with Matchbox cars, Star Wars action figures, and the board game Risk. She was also very involved at a young age in sports like soccer, field hockey, and lacrosse. Her reputation as a tomboy mostly protected her from negative comments from her peers, including those in her church. Her parents were not especially afraid that her tomboyishness meant anything in particular. As an adult, however, she recalled feeling different from other girls. She knew girls in sports, of course, but she felt different from most other girls, who seemed much more interested in playing with dolls or Barbies or playing house. She had no interest in these things. She refused to wear dresses and preferred shorts or jeans, T-shirts or sweatshirts. She remembered not fitting in with other girls her age.

Camila's experience is much like that of other sexual minorities. They often look back on their life and recall feeling different from their peers for reasons tied to their gender.

Making meaning out of same-sex sexuality. A person's first experience of same-sex attraction, and how they make sense of that experience, is a key milestone. This milestone usually occurs at puberty, at the same time that people who are straight report first experiencing attraction to the opposite sex.[7]

Young people navigating same-sex sexuality and faith have shared that the process of making sense of their attractions can include identity dissonance and confusion. For example, one college-aged student shared, "When I got into high school, I met someone [of the same sex], and I realized this is personal. This is me. This is my experience, and I feel this way about someone else. I don't fit into this mold of how everyone thinks I should be."[8]

For many Christian young people, their struggles with same-sex sexuality were focused on their religious faith. One person shared:

> It was hard every day, but many of those nights crying out to God . . . it was: "What is this? Why is this? What is its purpose? If this is a monster, why did God instill a monster within me? What kind of God would do that? God, I trust you, I believe in you, I love you, so why in the world would you do this to your child?"[9]

In our therapeutic offices, we can hear the anguish in young people of faith asking God about their sexuality and how to honor and trust him with it. This early wrestling can be a tender place for ministry, both as it is happening and in years to come. The balancing act of faith and sexuality becomes even more complicated when young people consider whether to share their experience with others.

Deciding whether to share their story. Deciding who to trust with their story of sexual identity and faith is an important and ongoing chapter in many people's lives. In digital and social media, coming out involves sharing and reworking identity, embodying and performing identity with peers—particularly those who have a common nonnormative identity.

Given what we have already said regarding the looping effect, many youth may not fully appreciate the impact of new and emerging taxonomies on their identity development since so much of identity is explored in online forums. They may not see the value of sharing with people in their in-person contexts and relationships.

When it comes to actually sharing about sexual orientation in face-to-face interactions, youth often listen for how others talk about sexual orientation more broadly to determine whether it would be safe to share their own experience. Deciding whether to share their story, then, centers on finding and accessing avenues of social support. This means identifying people they trust who can hold their story with respect and gentleness. Deciding whether to share their story also includes navigating private and public sexual identities. Private identity is how a person thinks of themself, while public identity is what they share with others or how they are known publicly.

Sharing their story with others, while helpful in some ways, can lead to confusion if no space is given for the possibility that this is an enduring reality, not just a phase. One interviewee shared with us:

> I was very convinced that I was not bisexual. . . . I talked about this with mom recently. I have tried to come out to her a dozen times between the ages of 10 and now. She would say [each time], "Oh it's just a phase." Then, hearing everybody else react about it, I was like, "Oh I'm not [bisexual]. I'm straight. I'm with a guy anyway. I'm not going to think about it."[10]

Another person we interviewed shared about the challenge of feeling guilty: "It was very much struggling with what that meant for who I was . . . within a family that didn't have much forgiveness. . . . I felt guilty almost all the time."[11]

Holding faith and sexuality. In our research, many sexual minority individuals say that one important chapter of their stories involved learning to "hold" both faith and sexuality as important parts of their life. Questioning God and questioning one's faith community are common themes in this chapter. For example, one person reflecting on his religious and spiritual struggles shared,

> I don't know that I would consider myself a Christian right now. I do believe in God and Jesus. Any form of organized religion . . . I just haven't found. It's not that I'm looking for acceptance, I'm just looking for something that makes sense of my experience, and I haven't felt that.[12]

Another person reflected on her "extremely conservative" and "fundamentalist" upbringing this way:

> [My upbringing] led me, like most of my peers, really to dislike the Christian faith as some legalistic, chauvinistic "better than you because I'm going to Heaven, and you're not" evidenced in the way you live/think thing. It was in late middle school and early high school that I decided to actually look at what the Christian faith was about, instead of what these people were telling me it was.[13]

In our research, we have described some people navigating sexual identity and faith as learning to hold these different aspects of themselves like two boxes that exist together, instead of rejecting one box or the other (see fig. 5.2).[14]

We have also seen other people compartmentalize their faith and sexual identities. Compartmentalizing means not being able at the moment to find a way to integrate or even to relate faith and sexuality. They are essentially kept at arm's length from one another. They do not have a relationship, even though both are important to a person. We see this compartmentalizing approach on display in a recent interview in which a young adult shared, "All I have is, like, just thoughts, possibilities [that] just kind of like float around, just kind of like there, and there's no integration. . . . I'm just kind of like floating."[15]

Here is another example of keeping faith and sexuality compartmentalized: "I guess at this point my sexual development is more at the forefront. . . . That's mostly because I've spent a lot of time thinking about my religious development, but until recently I had thought I was on the asexual spectrum, but now I realize that I'm not. . . . They [still] don't interact."[16]

Another person we interviewed reflected this kind of compartmentalization:

> [I am] starting to turn back to spiritual development. I am comfortable with my sexuality. I am just kind of comfortable with it and

Figure 5.2
Common ways people "hold" faith and sexuality

A. One Box: Integrated

Faith and sexuality are both important and integrated, and the person cannot speak of one without speaking of the other.

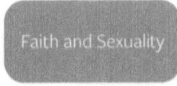

B. Box Within a Box: Integrated

Both faith and sexuality are important, and integration is achieved by placing one box inside the other, indicating that one has primacy over the other because it forms a boundary within which the other resides.

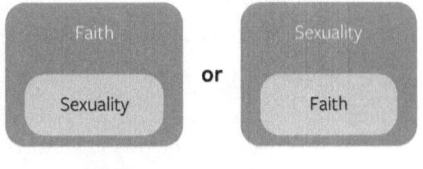

C. Two Boxes: Related

Faith and sexuality interact or relate, but neither is superior to the other.

D. Compartmentalization: Unrelated

Faith and sexuality are kept separate so that both boxes are present but do not interact.

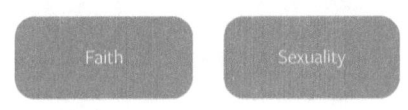

E. Rejecting: Unrelated

Either the sexuality box or the faith box is rejected.

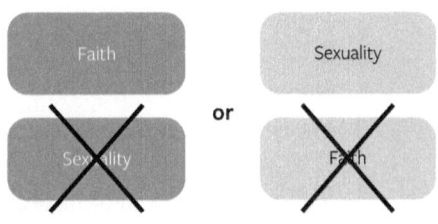

Adapted from Stratton et al., "Holding Faith and Sexual Identity Together."

done thinking about it. And so, I've noticed that I've become very cynical and I'm very tired of being cynical and hardened so I've started to look back towards . . . to focus on my religious identity.[17]

The integration or synthesis of faith identity and sexual identity can look different for different people. While some integrate these two identities by "holding" them like two boxes, as we described above, others resonate with the idea of holding one box rather than two; they feel that their faith identity and sexual identity are essentially inseparable.

Here's an example of a person describing their faith and sexuality as one box rather than two:

> I don't really see them as separate categories. I don't really perceive them in different categories because they are so intimately intertwined. Because it's out of my sexual development and my sexual understanding that I pursue intimacy with God. But it's also out of intimacy with God that I learn to better understand and integrate my sexuality. So it's hard for me to see one above the other or in a hierarchy, because they're just so . . . I don't know how to explain it. If that makes sense, they're both important because they're both ones that are important to me.[18]

Another integration strategy for faith and sexuality that we've seen in our interviews is to place one box within the other box. Religious faith and sexuality are both important, but one is placed within the bounds of the other. This means that one aspect of experience takes pride of place, and the other is subject to it. A person's sexuality can be bounded by their faith; alternatively, as in the following interview, religious faith may be placed within the bounds of sexual identity:

> I guess I wonder why same-sex attraction is treated the way it is in the Bible. I don't understand that, but I also know I can't believe that it's wrong when all of my experiences outside of that have

demonstrated otherwise. I know so many people, including myself, who are in stable, functional, healthy same-sex relationships.[19]

Some people have shared how, instead of placing one box inside the other, they hold two boxes. Both are equally important, and neither functions as the primary reference point for the other. This is another way of relating faith and sexuality:

> I would definitely say that they influence each other, certainly. The fact that I'm gay kinda influences where I want to go to church.... And I think something like that, where you have a safe community, is important in that way because it influences my religious life.[20]

In addition to all these approaches for holding the boxes of faith and sexuality together, we want to name one other approach for dealing with sexuality and faith: rejecting. In the posture of rejection, a person concludes that faith and sexuality cannot be held together: one has to be rejected for the person to believe they have found a way forward in life.

No matter what approach a person takes to reconciling sexual identity and faith, it seems to be universally true that sexuality is made more complex when we add religious faith to the story. Faith, in a sense, thickens the plot of sexual identity.

Living the story itself. This last part of the journey has to do with synthesizing sexual identity and fostering a sense of community. Sometimes people refer to this synthesis as identity achievement, suggesting an outcome that can be appreciated at the end of a long sojourn. This idea of achievement may feel accurate for some people, but it likely will not for everyone, especially not for adolescents and young adults. In our research, we have found that Christians often do not find resolution to the conflict they experience between their faith and their sexuality until somewhere between their mid- to late twenties and early to mid-thirties.[21] Regardless of how people hold the boxes of faith and sexuality, what does it look like for them to go on with life in the meantime?

Several themes emerge that could be helpful for young people who have often not resolved conflict as youth while still finding a way to move forward and grow. These include anchoring in a relationship with God through their journey, framing challenges along the way as opportunities for growth, and cultivating patience.

In this interview, a person shares about the way they find connection with God as an anchor as they navigate holding identity boxes. Their relationship becomes a resource and point of constancy in the midst of continued unknowns:

> I feel like this part of my identity is where I see God the most, if that makes sense. And a lot of times, I'm questioning, well am I using this to abuse his grace? No, I'm not. This is where he wants to show me himself. . . . It's almost like this is my connection to him. And I'm not saying that if it weren't for this in my life, I wouldn't be connected to him—I'm just saying that I've come to live and cope with a lot of things in my life and this is one way that I feel like I'm able to be myself before him.[22]

We can also see how someone is wrestling with what this holding could look like as they frame their journey as a process of learning and growing rather than judging what they call backtracking as a sign of failure as they live their story:

> [Now I'm] kind of backtracking and [being] like okay, what do like I actually, what do I want, or what do I feel like right is for me I guess. . . . You know not like in what do I want as in I'm going to do anything and . . . dodge the consequences or whatever, but more just like . . . is this actually something that I'm interested in, and what if it's not, and like what are the consequences of it, is that worth it? [I'm] learning to let what I want form my identity rather than my identity form what I want, you know . . . that's been the learning process over, and over, and over again.[23]

Cultivating patience is another principle that can be helpful in living the story itself. Thomas Acklin and Boniface Hicks give us insights into this important virtue:

> "Patience" comes from the Latin, *patior*, meaning "let it be done" as well as "to suffer" or "to be open." . . . We must choose to trust when familiar ways of presence disappear, and we are opened up to be able to receive the presence of God, which is silent, hidden, and mysterious.[24]

Forms of Life

As we round out a relational-narrative approach to ministry, we want to draw from the notion of *forms of life* from Ludwig Wittgenstein. This concept is a potentially helpful way to navigate tensions between orthodox Christians and the mainstream LGBTQ+ community.

Published posthumously in 1953, Wittgenstein's *Philosophical Investigations* explores how language is used, mentioning *Lebensformen*, or "forms of life." It is unclear what the precise meaning of *Lebensformen* is for Wittgenstein; however, it has been conceptualized as a shared way of living between individuals who have shared concepts, language, values, and cultural practices.[25]

Regarding a form of life, we imagine having a community of people who share language, concepts, values, and practices in a way that supports their members toward their sense of purpose and well-being. We suggest that there is—broadly speaking—a form of life reflected in the mainstream LGBTQ+ community, a set of shared beliefs, values, behaviors, language, labels, and assumptions often reflected in the mainstream of that community.

For the Christian, there is also a form of life we are to live. As followers of Christ, we are meant to share a set of beliefs, values, behaviors, language, labels, and assumptions that characterize us as a community. This is made difficult in part due to the controversies in ministry and the contrasting models for ministry. As Christians navigate emerging sexual identities and faith, we want to invite them by way of ministry into a form of life characteristic of the person of Christ and the work of the Holy Spirit. We want to acknowledge that while there will be some overlap between the mainstream LGBTQ+ form of life and the Christian form of life (perhaps when it comes to some labels used, for instance), there will also be places of distinction for the Christian who is a sexual minority (regarding beliefs, values, assumptions, and behaviors).

A Growth-Focused Form of Life

Rather than frame a ministry model solely around change (of orientation, identity, or behavior), as we discussed in chapter 4, we recommend a growth-focused model of ministry that can accompany our posture of cultural ambassadorship. While this model would be different in emphasis from each of the models discussed previously, it would share the hope of moving individuals toward greater Christian obedience and submission of self to the authority of Christ.

The growth-focused model we suggest emphasizes growth in Christ. Growth in Christ can be envisioned in remarkably different ways,[26] but we want to see a growth in Christ model characterized by self-acceptance (coming to terms with the reality of one's same-sex sexuality), grace to self (encountering the grace God has for a person), humility (less self-preoccupation), faith (trusting in God's provision), hope (the expectation that good will occur in time), and obedience to Christ.

The ministry model we are suggesting would listen for different ways people "hold" their sexual identity and their faith identity without having to leave one at the door. This approach allows young people to use familiar linguistic categories to communicate their current understanding of their sexuality, including the use of emerging sexual identity labels. It also allows youth to critically engage with queer theory in the context of Christian communities; parents, pastors, educators, and youth ministers are able to honor the aspects of queer theory that draw teens in while also cocreating a distinctively Christian form of life for youth to step into.

This being said, we may want to develop the idea of a Christian form of life with its own shared culture, language, values, and so on that integrates some facets and contrasts with other facets of the mainstream LGBTQ+ community.[27] This means that youth could *see* in their communities a path for them within integration of sexuality and faith.

Any form of living, including Christian living, involves shared culture, language, practices, values, mentors and spiritual guides, and a unified *telos*, or end that is sought after. Here's what it might look like to apply the Christian form of life approach to the sexuality conversation. We cocreate a community where language and practices integrate cultural dimensions of language and where Christian youth utilize labels that go beyond "same-sex attracted." We foster a form of life where youth can look up to adult Christian believers who see their sexual orientation as an important aspect of personhood while authentically living out their personhood in ways that seek after sexual stewardship. We witness Christians developing faith-congruent pastoral resources that reduce sexual shame and honor the unique challenges of queer-identifying youth. We cocreate supportive spaces for sexual minorities that are largely led by sexual minorities who model wisdom, clarity, courage, compassion, and grace.

We have seen all too many models who reject their faith for their sexuality or vice versa. We want to cultivate a vision that allows youth to embody and follow in the footsteps of other Christians who develop sustainable living within Christian communities. In practice, this could look like identifying sexual minority adults who can serve as mentors to sexual minority youth. This could mean inviting sexual minority adults to share with married people, single people, and broader faith communities about the wisdom they have gleaned from their journeys. This means identifying small group contexts in local faith communities and regional communities for sexual minorities to share with those within the LGBTQ+ umbrella and beyond it.

Even when youth are drawn to a range of labels to attempt to communicate about sexual orientation, they would then discover in Christian community distinctively Christian ways to talk about, engage with, and reflect their sexuality. This could involve a teen coming to your church's youth group and finding video resources readily available in which they witness sexual minorities robustly engaging sexuality. This could involve teens being given examples of adult sexual minorities cultivating sexual stewardship, with embodied examples that include single individuals as well as those in mixed-orientation marriages. This could include youth taking steps to develop their own spaces in their schools and churches to serve marginalized communities out of a desire to cultivate belonging and reduce the alienation others feel.

Concluding Thoughts

As we close this chapter on a relational-narrative approach to ministry, we recognize you may have emerging questions as you try to consider the nuances around walking with youth holding their sexuality and faith in various ways.

As a reminder, here is a list of the distinct ways a youth may be holding sexuality and faith as they navigate their sexual identity journey. We recommend a deeper study of these holding patterns and their implications for ministry:

A. Faith and sexuality are both important and integrated, and the person cannot speak of one without speaking of the other (one box).

B. Faith and sexuality are important, and integration is achieved by placing faith inside sexuality, indicating that sexuality has primacy over faith (a box within a box).

B. Faith and sexuality are important, and integration is achieved by placing sexuality inside faith, indicating that faith has primacy over sexuality (a box within a box).
C. Faith and sexuality interact or relate, but neither is superior to the other (two boxes).
D. Faith and sexuality are kept separate, so that the faith and sexuality boxes are present but do not interact (compartmentalizing).
E. Faith has been rejected because this feels necessary to find a way forward in life (rejecting).
E. Sexuality has been rejected because this feels necessary to find a way forward in life (rejecting).

In light of the complexity that emerges here in relational ministry, we advise taking time to pray, jot down ideas, and discuss the following questions with others in your community seeking to accompany today's youth:

- What are three helpful principles and three challenges that would come up as you walk with a person whose holding patterns vary in the distinct ways mapped in this chapter?
- What is a concrete way to navigate each of the challenges you might encounter?

We believe your effort at engaging personally and communally in the above reflections can help equip you to better anticipate the challenges and opportunities available in your ministry to youth whose holding patterns will vary. Further, we trust these reflections will create space for developing concrete insights to help buffer against these challenges as we seek to overcome barriers to relational-narrative ministry.

CHAPTER 6

Narrative Revisited

Minister to Questions Tied to Chapters in a Life Story

In chapter 5, we discussed the key experiences in the development of sexual identity from a narrative perspective. These include preface (gender atypicality in childhood), initial attractions and corresponding meaning, disclosure to others (coming out), holding the boxes (relating sexuality and faith), and living the story itself (achieving a kind of synthesis). Let's take a look at the questions tied to chapters in a young person's narrative and begin to think about how we might listen well to those questions as they arise in ministry or parenthood.

To get a practical sense for the questions tied to chapters in a person's narrative, we will highlight three different youth—Carla, Anton, and Ty—to unpack specific ministry approaches with different young people in the various chapters of their lives.

Carla is a fifteen-year-old Latina Catholic teen who began to notice attraction to other girls right around puberty. She attended Catholic school but never heard anyone speak much about people who identify as bisexual or queer, which are labels she would use. When she is with certain friends, she talks openly about her crushes on girls. When she is with her family and youth group peers, she is much more hesitant to acknowledge this aspect of her story.

Anton is a sixteen-year-old African American nondenominational Christian. He first became aware of his sexual attraction to men at twelve and decided to disclose it to his youth minister at fourteen. He got the sense that his church community could receive him in this experience, and he continued to share about his sexuality more publicly as his high school years unfolded.

Ty is a seventeen-year-old white teen who attends a Pentecostal church. He came out as biromantic to his older sister at sixteen, only because she was no longer a Christian. He felt immense shame about his sexuality, so he compartmentalized it. He felt like he had no other choice.

Gender Atypicality

Regarding gender atypicality in childhood, many young people who express an emerging sexual identity are asking, "Am I normal?" It's important to anticipate this question from youth and how you might want to answer it, both explicitly and implicitly.

On the surface, nonnormative sexualities do not reflect the norm (by definition). In that sense, a young person who reflects an emerging sexual identity does not reflect the societal norms for sexual identity insofar as those norms are heterosexual/straight.

When a youth is asking, "Am I normal?" it is important for us to be aware that, on the surface, the answer is different across residual, dominant, and emergent taxonomies.

- Residual: "No, you are abnormal and either sinful or mentally ill."
- Dominant: "Yes, you are normal; that was the point of liberation and assimilationist approaches—to be included in mainstream culture."

- Emergent: "Who cares? What is deemed 'normal' is a social construct used to perpetuate injustice and inequality."

Self-acceptance as an alternative to rigid taxonomies. Rather than declare yes or no to the question "Am I normal?" from the vantage point of one of the three taxonomies we have been discussing throughout this book, a good angle of entry into questions about what is normal is to move past that question and focus instead on attuning to and responding to the deeper questions of young people.

One of the deeper questions of young people, beneath the normalcy question, is how to find self-acceptance and belonging in community. In our research, we have seen the importance of self-acceptance in helping sexual minority young adults improve their mental health and well-being.[1] "Self-acceptance" can be a misleading term, because it is often used to imply that a person has moved toward a stance that affirms same-sex sexual behavior. However, this is not what we mean by self-acceptance, nor does self-acceptance necessarily involve affirmation of same-sex sexual behavior in the research we have done. As I (Mark) have written elsewhere:

> Often when people think about self-acceptance for sexual minorities, they assume this means accepting one's sexuality *and* affirming same-sex relationships. Our research, though, suggests that self-acceptance may be the acceptance of one's sexuality regardless of one's moral position about sexuality. It seems that sexual minorities with more traditionally orthodox views of sexuality can find self-acceptance just as those who affirm same-sex relationships, although the process may take a bit longer in the case of the former.[2]

So, what *is* self-acceptance?

A hallmark of self-acceptance is that a young person accepts all parts of themselves, even those parts that are not valued by themself or by others in their communities. They are receptive to the "good" and "bad" parts of themself. For example, a teen can be receptive to the reality that they experience attraction, even if they see the attraction as something to be held at arm's length due to shame or something to be stewarded in such a way where they do not engage in sexual activity with someone of the same sex. Or a teen may discover ways to practice bodily acceptance or neutrality around their body and pray for a greater sense of love for themselves even as they struggle with their self-image in adolescence.

Self-acceptance is related to grace to self. Grace to self is a "trait that reflects the way people make space for grace in relation to their own self-experience." Put differently, grace to self is "grace applied to the ways in which people manage themselves, as an intrapersonal, acceptance-based process within [themselves]."[3]

So, to a youth like Carla, Anton, or Ty asking, "Am I normal?" we could say:

> When people ask that question, often they are asking deeper questions, like "Am I wanted?"; "Do I belong?"; "Will you accept me?"; and "Is there a place for me in the body of Christ?" In our community, you are wanted and you do belong. There is a place for you here. In this place, we want to help you come to terms with the reality of your sexuality and explore in this community how to honor God with your desires. We want to support you as you come to terms with the reality of your sexuality, and my hope is that you would experience God's love for you deeply as you work to accept this reality.

Self-acceptance as a way to attend to shame. One consideration in promoting self-acceptance is that this will likely also help address shame. We shared in chapter 5 that many people navigating Christian faith and same-sex sexuality experience toxic shame, and in the example of Ty we see this very clearly.

With regard to experiencing shame, Ty's youth minister, mentors, therapist, and parents can help him in extending grace in how he thinks about himself (i.e., noticing and replacing unhelpful, shaming thoughts and self-talk with more helpful, self-accepting thoughts) and how he emotionally experiences himself (using imagery in prayer and therapy that invites God's compassion in the places of self-rejection and shame).

The best thing we can suggest for ministering to shame is to model age- and role-appropriate openness, as this is an antidote for toxic shame. It may not be appropriate to be particularly open about the specifics of your deeper struggles to youth; we understand that. But we do not want to come across as being perfect or creating such a gap between where a person is (in terms of shame) and where they perceive you to be (in terms of perfection). Think of ways you can be more honest and transparent that reflect a more realistic image of who you are rather than an idealized image of who you are.

You could share with a youth navigating shame, for instance, that you also have feelings of shame at times in your walk with Jesus (thoughts that you are bad, defective, or unworthy) and are actively seeking ways to approach Jesus with those facets of yourself that hold shame. You could also model grace to self by sharing a way that you are learning to offer tenderness in response to a weakness in your life, great or small. Grace to self and authentic openness are especially important in Christian settings that prefer testimonies of perfection, where the pressure may otherwise fall on people to appear exempt from weakness.

Another powerful way to promote self-acceptance and reduce shame is to talk in honoring ways about Christian sexual minorities. When you give examples of people growing in Christlikeness, include people who have similar characteristics and experiences as sexual minority youth. Refrain from giving examples of sexual minorities only as spiritually deficient. Speak positively and matter-of-factly about the reality that sexual minorities exist and are part of young people's social world at school and in digital and social media. Talking in this way will help sexual minority youth feel known and seen even if they have never disclosed this part of their experience to you.

We also want to be clear with youth that we do not think their pattern of sexual attraction (or lack of sexual attraction) is a matter of willful disobedience on their part. While we do not know what causes attractions to the same sex, we do not believe that a person simply makes a decision to have the attractions they experience. Unfortunately, statements like "homosexuality is a sin" are often understood as a condemnation of people attracted to the same sex. The term "homosexuality" is so imprecise; it might refer to attraction, behavior, identity, or orientation. When we use the residual language of "homosexuality," we are not only speaking a language that feels strange to youth raised in dominant categories and steeped in emergent taxonomies; we are also being imprecise in ways that will leave some young people feeling condemned and leave others more likely to write off both you and the faith you represent.

Attractions and Meaning

When we think about initial attractions and meaning making, the question is "How do I make sense of my same-sex sexuality?" The search for meaning is what I (Mark) have elsewhere referred to as an "attributional search" for identity.[4] To what do they attribute their same-sex sexuality? How do they think of their identity in light of their sexuality and Christian faith? This is a meaning-making process that takes time.

We have not found it helpful to merely tell young people how to make meaning of their sexuality and faith, as though we could dictate those terms to them or as though our relationship is contingent on them accepting our preferred pathway of making meaning.

This approach will come across as top-down and controlling, and it is rarely effective long-term. To say we don't prescribe meaning for sexual minorities doesn't mean we advise Christian ministers or parents to discard sexual ethics or refrain from sharing about faith-congruent pathways for making meaning of sexual attraction. We simply advise creating space for teens to consider various paths of meaning making instead of forcing them to choose your preferred pathway or else risk losing a relationship with you.

In our role as clinicians, we have found that the best way to facilitate a teen's attributional search for meaning is to ask good questions. We recommend a similar approach to those in ministry, even as we recognize that ministry conversations will also likely include themes of morality, virtue, sin, and repentance. Many ministers will feel a moral responsibility to teach and guide in a more directive way, especially with youth. We hold a similar tension in our own roles in ministry. From a developmental perspective, we recognize that youth need guidance and space to discern with those guides. If we occupy the space of answers or directives, it is hard for teens to occupy that space for themselves and take in our feedback. The more prescriptive that adults tend to be with teens in an authoritarian way, the more teens will likely push back or resist. Thus, a more open manner of curiosity allows a teen to take increasing responsibility for their spiritual journey while feeling scaffolded by those who hold spiritual responsibility for accompaniment as well. We can hold hopes, high expectations, and belief in a teen's capacity for making meaning in Christlike ways while also holding out high warmth, curiosity, and openness in the process.

Facilitating a teen's search for meaning will certainly include challenging them at times within the context of a supportive relationship. In the case of Carla, it might mean digging deeper into her questions about sexual relationships and helping her wrestle more deeply with a Christian vision for sexuality. It involves allowing Carla, and any teen, to ask hard questions, disagree with you, and push back on your ideas. This kind of back-and-forth is best done in a relationship of deep trust, where a teen knows that disagreement does not lead to rejection.

Imagine if Carla had asked her youth minister or pastor, "How am I supposed to make sense of my sexuality in light of my faith? Am I supposed to deny this part of me and follow Jesus? Am I allowed to be in a relationship with someone of the same sex if I end up wanting that? Or does obedience demand that I be single?"

It's helpful for a minister to validate the gravity of these questions. We could imagine a minister saying, "These are such important questions, questions that are fair game to bring to God and to trusted supports in the church. God is not surprised or scrambling for a plan B for your life as you ask these questions. He has a good plan for you, even if you don't know all the details yet."

In questions about what it looks like to be obedient to Christ, another principle that often arises is self-denial. We can hold that life in Christ certainly involves self-denial and obedience. In that way, Christianity is markedly different from approaches that see self-indulgence as authenticity and freedom. And yet, God does not ask us to exile parts of ourselves and sever off aspects of our experience outright. While he will invite us into discernment of how to live with our particular experiences, he does not require us to reject or suppress sexual desire in and of itself.

When questions about sexual relationships arise, it's valuable to recognize that Christianity informs how we answer these questions. A Christian vision for sexuality looks different from other visions because God has a plan for our sexuality and cares deeply about how we live out every facet of our lives, including in the realm of sexual expression. At the same time, if our teens are not compelled by the thought of lifelong singleness, for instance, we can normalize that this hesitancy is understandable. We can invite God into their questions rather than immediately launching into a lecture about the morality of same-sex sexual relationships simply because a person brings up their longing for such a relationship.

Disclosure to Others

As sexual minority youth, like Anton, begin to share their story with others, they are asking the question, "Whom can I trust with my story?" As Christian ministers or parents, we want to *be* trustworthy in a way that creates room for young people to share difficult things with us. We never ask a person to trust us before we demonstrate our trustworthiness.

Note that the trustworthiness we demonstrate will increase the likelihood that they will trust us with their experience of their sexuality and sexual identity. Here are some ways you can demonstrate your trustworthiness to young people:

- Be respectful to them.
- Value the relationship you have with them.
- Be clear in your communication.
- Listen well.
- Hold what is shared in confidence.
- Admit mistakes when you make them.
- Stay engaged over time.

If a teen shares more about their sexuality or sexual identity with you—if they "come out"—thank them for trusting you with that part of their experience.

Keep in mind that disclosure and the response you offer could easily be contrasted in the mind of an adolescent or young adult with the celebratory approach available to them in the mainstream LGBTQ+ community. We want to offer another way to think about responding as Christians. This draws from the best of what youth encounter in mainstream LGBTQ+ contexts and does so in distinctively Christian ways (see table 6.1).

Some youth may feel concerned about coming out in faith settings. Other youth will wonder, "What's the big deal?" because they are so immersed in a world of emerging sexual and gender

Table 6.1
Responses to Disclosure

Mainstream LGBTQ+ Response	Recommended Ministry Response
Pride	Empathic receptivity
Visibility	Respect
Solidarity	Compassion
Self-actualization	Self-acceptance
Celebration	Grace for self
Collectivity	Community

identities. They may have no frame of reference for why sexual identity could be a point of tension for you or anyone else.

For Christian parents, mentors, and ministers who want to be receptive to a young person's disclosure, we recommend cultivating a response we call "empathic receptivity." This empathic response is characterized by *respect* for the person disclosing and *compassion* for the challenges they are facing. At the same time, we want to refrain from responding in a way that is condescending or insinuates that we feel sorry for the young person. This moves us out of pathologizing approaches and toward a more robust ministry approach. It can sound like this:

> I admire your courage in sharing your experience of sexuality with me. I want to hear more about what it's been like to navigate sexuality questions in our community. Thank you for trusting me. I trust God is going to continue to work beautiful things through your life in and through your experience of sexuality. I can't wait to witness what he has in store for you in your walk with him.

An empathic response should facilitate *self-acceptance* of all aspects of a person, including those parts that may not be valued in some settings:

> God sees you and knows you intimately. He invites you to bring all parts of yourself to him, including your sexual desires and

experiences. He does not ask that you pretend you don't experience same-sex attraction [or, in the case of a person identifying as asexual, pretend that you experience sexual attraction] for you to approach him. Sometimes in our faith communities, we struggle to honor people's experiences of attraction or lack of attraction, and sometimes in the mainstream queer culture, a person's faith is discounted. Self-acceptance of all the parts of ourselves can be difficult, but it's something we want to cultivate here.

This response should help promote *grace for self*. It should bring the youth into *community* rather than drive them away from community. Rather than telling a youth not to talk about their sexuality with others, we want to encourage them to identify trustworthy people who can journey with them:

> I am so grateful you are part of our community. I want to be one of several people in your circle who can accompany you on your journey of faith. That involves being honest with trustworthy people. You are not alone in having this experience, and you belong in our community. There's nowhere else I'd rather you be. There can be challenges along the way navigating faith and sexuality, and I hope you find a home here to walk this out.

In order to facilitate self-acceptance, we may need to help youth with disclosure to others, such as parents. You can provide them with support and suggested language for sharing their experience. Like we have mentioned previously, you can help them consider the use of descriptive and "person-first" language, such as "I experience same-sex sexuality and am sorting out what that means." For youth for whom English is a second language for some family members, it will be especially important to consider how to use language to discuss orientation with loved ones.

Within the big ideas that the LGBTQ+ community has communicated about coming out responses, we recognize that these can be done very well (in line with Jesus) or poorly (in contradiction to our faith), and we want to show you a distinctively Christian way of responding. Whether we consider National Coming Out Day in October or the celebration of Pride Month in June, both are intended to reflect the *visibility* of the LGBTQ+ community, along with *solidarity*, *celebration*, and *collectivity*. *Pride* is marked by the celebration of sexual expression as a sign of freedom. The celebratory response fosters collectivity, often captured in the colloquial reference to the LGBTQ+ community as a "family." *Self-actualization* of oneself, of one's sexuality, is underscored and supported in a collective manner that many people who experience same-sex sexuality find meaningful in terms of elevating their status in a society that has historically devalued them through residual taxonomies, either religious or psychiatric.

Christian ministry approaches, at their best, will offer a pathway of true freedom for sexual minority youth, which can be distinguished from the pathway offered by secular pride, without sacrificing anything good within that community. Thus, responding to disclosure in a distinctively Christian way allows us to uphold the dignity of sexual minority youth, believe in their capacity to experience freedom as a beloved child of God within a Christian vision for marriage and sexuality, and cultivate and communicate their belonging in the church community resolutely and ongoingly.

Holding Sexuality and Faith

Another question youth often wrestle with in relating sexual identity and religious identity is, "How do I hold my same-sex sexuality and my faith?" The holding patterns we discussed in chapter 5 may be more relevant to youth ministry than the letters that designate theological positions (such as Side A and Side B). While we believe that theological positions are important, getting a fourteen-year-old to declare the right position is not really ministry. A tidy approach that focuses on teens' intellectual assent to certain beliefs during their time in youth ministry can unfortunately become a distraction from true ministry to young people, many of whom will be on a journey of wrestling with these beliefs through adolescence. In contrast, the model of *holding patterns* can be a metaphor that helps teens grapple with their experiences and their faith both now and in the years to come.

Recall that the common ways people hold faith and sexuality are (see fig. 5.2):

- One box: integrated
- A box within a box: integrated
- Two boxes: related
- Compartmentalization: unrelated
- Rejecting: unrelated

This model can be a helpful ministry and counseling tool when you begin to walk with someone. You can simply introduce the metaphor, offer a brief description of various ways of holding faith and sexuality, and then ask them what they think: "Which way of holding your faith and sexuality resonates with you right now?"

We want to turn now to highlighting how Carla, Anton, and Ty are navigating holding patterns differently. Each requires a nuanced ministry approach.

Carla was asked this question in a therapy session one afternoon. She teared up at the question and spoke to how she has felt forced into rejecting one box thus far:

> I didn't know there was any way other than rejecting one box or the other. I've often been told by my parents that I need to "choose God above all else," which has made me feel terrible for even considering holding the sexuality box at all and acknowledging my bisexuality. I like the idea of having two boxes that are related, but I can't even imagine integrating them. I guess I'll hold out hope that it could be possible, but I just can't picture it.

Anton shared with his youth leader about his own way of holding his sexuality and faith as two boxes that are related:

> My first thought is that I hold these boxes as two related ones, because I attend a group at my public high school for those who identify in the LGBT umbrella, and I also am pretty involved in my youth group. In both settings, I can talk about the other aspect. In the LGBT group at school, everyone knows me as the "queer guy who loves Jesus more than anything and doesn't party or hook up," and in my youth group, I can share about my experience of being gay and how it impacts my life. There, I can also share struggles with gay pornography with trustworthy people who are helping me with understanding God's mercy and grace to help me with that.

Ty shared that, when he first came out as biromantic, he had compartmentalized his faith and sexuality. This posture shifted over time:

> Now, I see my faith and sexuality as a box within a box. My sexuality fits in the box of my faith, which to me doesn't mean that my sexuality matters less but that everything within me can be contained within my relationship with God. He receives all of me in the embrace of his love and knows that I don't have my future figured out with it all yet. But I trust him to hold this sexuality box with me. On days that I feel stressed about how it all fits, I know that he will hold the sexuality box for me, within my walk with him.

In ongoing ministry with young people, you can refer back to the analogy of holding patterns to empathically reflect on what you see in their attempts to hold these aspects of themselves. Just as we read in the example of Ty above, youth may use different approaches over the course of their time in counseling or ministry. It is not uncommon to see movement across holding patterns over time. It helps for ministers, therapists, and parents to be curious and to keep asking questions about how young people are holding these aspects of their experience. Be respectful of both sexuality and faith. Offer encouragement and admiration at a young person's courageous attempts to hold and honor these aspects of themself.

The good news is this: We don't have to choose between being empathetic and validating or teaching and directing. We can keep doctrine in view, and articulate that doctrine in clear, calm, and compassionate conversations, while we also focus on helping the person make meaning of their faith as they ask difficult questions, pointing them with our own lives to the only person who can answer those questions. We also trust that the Holy Spirit is at work and will be guiding them into all truth.

Put differently, we want those we accompany to have their own relationship with the Father and to be able to have an ongoing conversation with him in which they can ask difficult questions and wrestle with any answers they receive, including conclusions they may draw when they hear silence. We model for them with our own lives the virtue of patience.

We mentioned patience in the previous chapter as a virtue God cultivates in sexual minority young people. We can ask God to help us, too, with patience when we are creating space for young people to hold their faith and sexuality. The people we will minister to will be using different ways of holding these over many years. Your role may not be one in which you see the entire arc of how they hold their faith and sexuality. Rather, be familiar with the holding patterns so you can recognize them in a youth you are ministering to. Then ask yourself, "Given that she is holding her faith and sexuality this way, what is she going to need from me this next month (or six months, or twelve months)?"

Living the Story

For many sexual minorities, a final key question as they live out the story of their sexual identity and faith is, "What does congruence look like for me?" As we discussed in chapter 5, "congruence" refers to a person living their life and forming an identity out of a counternarrative beyond celebration or abomination.

For Carla, who initially felt she had to reject either her sexuality or her faith to find a path forward, finding congruence at the end of high school meant deciding to break up with a girlfriend she had been dating and be single as she entered college. She wanted space to focus on her education and explore what it could look like to foster an undistracted relationship with God while still identifying as queer. She still wasn't sure of her beliefs about same-sex relationships, but she wanted to grow closer to God as she continued to explore Scripture and what path she would take in the future.

For Anton, who had held his faith identity and sexual identity like two related boxes that weren't integrated, finding congruence meant continuing to grow in his ability to live in accordance with his values. He made it his aim to abstain from same-sex sexual behavior and pornography use, even though he sometimes still hoped to one day fall in love with a man. He gradually felt like he had only one box: his life and walk with God. His sexuality was now included in that box and didn't require a separate box anymore, though he was still involved in different communities where one aspect of his experience was understood more than another.

For Ty, who continued to find value in having a box within a box, he often went back and forth in his beliefs about sexual behaviors. Congruence for him meant trusting that God was with him even when he felt angry at God for his experience of sexual attraction. He grew in grace to self, which allowed him to less frequently feel the need to compartmentalize these aspects of himself in prayer and community.

Each of these stories of congruence represents a progression, without an element of finality or everything being tied up with a bow.

Concluding Thoughts

In this chapter, we recommended ways in which ministry to teens can be tied to the chapters in the book of their lives. Much of what is occurring developmentally is pointing young people to a kind of congruence as they navigate emerging sexual and gender identities and religious faith.

As youth move through these developmental periods, these chapters in their own lives, some teens may feel pressure, from themselves or others, to have a definitive approach to congruence etched in stone for now and all time. We recommend that you help remove this pressure by normalizing the idea of ongoing personal growth.[5] Their efforts at personal congruence can be a rough draft that is still being edited, reworked, and revised.

We turn now to some final recommendations for ministry to youth as we consider additional thoughts for care and counseling.

CHAPTER 7

Engaging Youth

Ministry Recommendations for Care and Counseling

Lana, a fifteen-year-old Korean American teen, came to her first youth night at a local nondenominational church after moving to the area. She identifies as graysexual and bicurious. By "graysexual," she means that she has experienced sexual and romantic attraction but not to the degree she hears about from peers who experience attraction. For Lana, "bicurious" means that she is still exploring whether she could be attracted to men and/or women in the future.

Lana was raised Christian and still shares with her friends that she is a Christian, but she is skeptical about youth group spaces. She's heard in her online chat rooms—which are mostly made up of queer-identifying youth—that most Christians think of queer people as "a problem to be solved." She is interested in learning more about God and seeing what it means to be a Christian, especially since she is so close to her grandmother, whose faith she has always admired. At the same time, she doesn't quite know how to square her faith with her sexual orientation. She doesn't expect there to be "much space for me as I am."

The faith community Lana is stepping into—including staff, youth mentors, and some peers—is likely drawing from residual categories and terms like "homosexuality," viewing same-sex attraction as primarily a spiritual or psychological problem. Lana herself is adopting emergent sexual identity labels that flow from emergent categories. Sadly, stories like this one often unfold all too predictably.

Specific Ministry Recommendations

We now turn to specific recommendations for ministry. We recommend that youth ministers and other laypeople walking with LGBTQ+ young people minister to the person rather than the label, emphasize a sustained relationship, cocreate a ministry climate that is emotionally and spiritually secure, and offer discipleship (see fig. 7.1).

- Minister to the person rather than the label
- Emphasize a sustained relationship
- Cocreate a ministry climate that is emotionally and spiritually secure
- Offer discipleship

Walking with youth navigating sexual identity and faith

Figure 7.1 Ministry recommendations: emerging sexual identities

Minister to the Person Rather Than the Label

We described three postures in chapter 4: culture warriors, cultural capitulators, and cultural ambassadors. As cultural ambassadors, we recognize varying preferences for different taxonomies while remaining curious as to how language functions for the person we are ministering to, all while thoughtfully challenging aspects of cultural trends that depart from a Christian worldview. This allows for critical engagements with cultural trends as we seek to understand them more fully *with* youth. Allowing ourselves to be formed as cultural ambassadors will help us minister to the person rather than to changing labels, because it invites us into a nonreactive space. It allows us to be proactive in our engagement, not shrinking at the opportunity to engage culture but feeling courageous and eager to do so.

What barriers might get in the way of you ministering to the person? We find that a common barrier for ministers is our own emotional reactivity. These emotions might include fear, anger, protectiveness, disgust, confusion, and apathy. Another barrier is when ministers assume a young person is aligned with political activism and react to them as a political enemy rather than responding to them as a person sharing their story. Finding places to process your emotions will be important, especially if you find yourself feeling reactive to youth navigating these identity questions. Finally, just as we talk about how youth are shaped by their exposure to media, sometimes our own exposure to media sources makes us less equipped to respond calmly and thoughtfully to the youth that Christ is inviting us into relationship with.

Moving Beyond Culture War Rhetoric

In ministry to the person, we want to elevate ministry above culture wars and above any politically motivated positioning. We do this in part so that we are not reactive to developments around sexual identity labels, as we have seen with younger people being drawn to emerging sexual identity taxonomies. We are not to be pro-gay (or any emergent sexual identity) or anti-gay (or any emergent sexual identity). We are advocates for the image of God in all people. We rise above culture wars and refuse to descend into simplistic pro-/anti- framings of these issues. How do we do this?

We remain committed to ministering to the person rather than to the label. We express this commitment less by *saying* it and more by *showing* it. We listen for labels, expressing respect and curiosity about how labels function for people. At the same time, we seek to build a relationship with a person, who cannot be reduced to labels, regardless of whether they adopt those labels or not.

When we minister to the person and not the label, we don't need to defend residual or dominant taxonomies against the rise of emergent taxonomies. These contrasting taxonomies are the result of myriad social and cultural factors. You may draw primarily from one taxonomy (for example, residual) over another (for example, emergent), but there is little gained in defending one of these taxonomies in and of itself. Defending a preferred taxonomy is not ministry; it is an intellectual exercise that will likely be lost on the young person standing in front of you, especially if this is the extent of your engagement. We want you to be familiar with a variety of possible taxonomies so you can position yourself to minister to a variety of people.

Addressing Labels Without Getting Stuck There

Being familiar with various taxonomies is important in part because people will likely ask you about the taxonomy of your ministry (though they probably won't use that language). They may ask what language you use when you discuss sexuality and faith with young people. We advise explaining your approach by saying that you want to help the young person in front of you navigate questions of sexual identity and faith.[1] This descriptive frame helps you refrain from immediately prescribing labels to your youth, but it also keeps you from turning a blind eye to the reality of sexuality and identity questions.

It's also worth noting that many youth will choose to adopt sexual identity labels regardless of whether you prescribe them, reject them, or remain neutral. We observed in chapter 4 that young people may also code switch in your presence: That is, they'll adopt your preferred language when they are with you and use their preferred language or that of their peers when they are not. To be more nuanced about the meaning of labels, we can keep in mind the distinctions between identity language, the attractions and orientation that are suggested in the use of identity terminology, possible behaviors, and so on. These are all different aspects of a young person's frame of reference for understanding their sexuality, and they could use labels to describe one or all of these aspects. All of these aspects can feel entangled, hierarchized, or unrelated in a young person's mind or experience, and part of ministry may be to help them disentangle one from another and discern each one independently. We can give youth permission to share and discuss their own wondering about what their attractions mean about identity while making space for them to be on a journey where they are exploring this in real time. Some youth will use a term to describe their orientation without seeing it as the most formative aspect of identity.

Consider the example of Lana at the start of this chapter. In Lana's case, ministry to the person rather than the label means accounting for her experience of sexuality within the context of her sense of self more broadly. It means getting to know Lana's interests, strengths, passions, fears, difficulties, and hopes. When she discloses about her understanding of sexuality, this ministry approach will ask questions about that aspect of her experience and how it fits within her faith while continuing to see her as more than *solely* a sexual minority person and getting to know her holistically.[2]

Sometimes, in the hopes of not fixating on sexual orientation conversations or out of fear of saying "the wrong thing," Christian ministers will refrain from talking about that aspect of experience at all. Being unwilling to talk with teens about sexuality can come across as rejecting, even if it's well-intentioned. Here are some ways to ask about sexuality in the context of ministry to the person, instead of ignoring the labels a teen uses or pretending there is nothing to be understood behind those labels:

- Thanks for sharing about your sexuality with me. I have heard that term you used before, but I know it can mean different things to different people sometimes. How do you understand that term?
- What about that term resonated with you when you first learned about it?
- Some people use sexual identity language to signal the most central piece of their identity, while others see their sexual desires as just one part of their broader identity. Right now, how do you understand the relationship between your sexuality and the rest of who you are?

Notice the use of the phrase "right now" to ask about a youth's understanding. The purpose of these words is not to imply a teen is merely going through a phase. Rather, we want to create space for their self-understanding to unfold over time. This keeps teens from feeling pigeonholed into one way of thinking or acting forever. If a teen is currently using a label to indicate that their sexuality has the primary significance in their sense of identity, we recommend not arguing this point directly with them. Instead, hold on to your own holistic understanding of this teen and reinforce other parts of their identity that are important (including their faith identity). We want to strike the balance of making space to talk about sexuality without fixating on it at the expense of the whole person.

Emphasize a Sustained Relationship

Youth ministries in the last thirty years have increasingly formalized and regimented their processes. Some have moved toward using a range of metrics—including attendance, service engagement, retention from year to year, and ongoing church attendance after students graduate from high school—to gauge their ministry effectiveness. While these metrics can be beneficial, we wonder if at times they distract us from the relational components of our ministry. Teens can tell when we are genuinely invested in their wellness. We want to be attentive to the situations our teens encounter within and outside of our faith community walls, committing to walk out their lives with them to whatever extent God asks us.

A recent review of the available research on the mental health of sexual minorities has shown the value that relationships sustained over time have for youth mental health.[3] These sustained relationships may be with parents and youth leaders, but they can also be with youth and other healthy supports. The quality of such relationships can be both risk factors and protective factors for sexual minority youth.

There are three primary categories of relationship, in addition to parents, that impact youth mental health, for good or ill, depending on the quality of the relationships:

- Peer relationships
- Faith community relationships
- Cultural community[4]

Even though most youth ministers engage primarily with youth themselves, they can also have a substantial indirect influence on teens through the ways they engage with parents, influence their broader faith community climate to foster belonging for youth, and help cultivate relationships between youth peers.

To this day, effective youth leaders will receive calls and visits from youth (now adults) they have mentored in youth ministry. These young adults reach out to ask questions about everything from mental health to faith to family circumstances. They reach out not because they necessarily agree with everything their leader has shared with them about faith over the years or because they all currently practice their Christian faith, but rather because they felt genuinely known, loved, and supported by the leader. And when they have spiritual questions in particular, years later, we hope they have found in you a reliable guide to point them back to Christ. This is perhaps the most helpful metric for how your ministry is doing with sustained relationship building.

Family Relationships

A key area that can negatively impact youth mental health is high conflict with parents. For sexual minority youth, conflict often forms around the milestone events we covered in chapter 5, including disclosure and sexual behaviors. If teens are navigating high-conflict relationships with parents, it is valuable to have referrals to local therapists who can assist with these situations. We have seen the value in youth groups bringing in mental health professionals from the community to give talks, share information, and train youth staff.

Along with connecting families to community resources, we recommend supporting open lines of communication between teens and parents rather than engaging them totally separately. You don't want a teen to foster a connection with you at the expense of their relationship with their parents. This could mean checking in with parents, with the teen's permission, after a youth discloses their sexual orientation/exploration. This could mean listening to a teen vent about parents and offering validation of the difficulties they are facing at home while also acknowledging the ways the parent or caregiver might be expressing protectiveness and love in their approach. It could also mean helping a teen consider ways to share about their sexual attraction with their parents in a way that accounts for the residual taxonomy their parents may be drawing from. (For instance, a teen might want to start a conversation with their parents by using descriptive language like "not experiencing sexual or romantic attraction" as opposed to emergent language such as "ace" or "asexual.")

Faith Community Relationships

Understanding and helping shape a teen's experience of the local church is another way to help improve the relationships they are accessing in church, protect against mental health difficulties, and foster resilience. In your ministry role, you will be a part of the local church and a powerful witness. And yet, members of different church communities can be diverse both in their theological convictions and in their ministry approach with sexual minority youth. As we mentioned in chapter 4, some ministry leaders and attendees may be drawn to the change of orientation approach, while others may be focused more on change of behavior or change of identity.

For starters, it's worth unpacking with a teen how they experience the broader community. This will help adults begin to support a teen in locating good mentors/connections with whom to form deeper relationships and steering clear of those who may be less helpful. We think of this as helping youth identify and access "pockets of safety" within a context rather than opting in or out of the context completely. Adults can begin by discussing sexuality more openly with church members and staff to identify potential mentors for youth. Further, when we identify adults who can be trustworthy, we can ask about their openness to mentor youth. We can even begin to set up streamlined pathways for adults to be identified as mentors to youth, highlighting those who are equipped to walk with sexual minority youth.

At the same time, we will want to help a teen consider and anticipate the various trickle-down messages they will interact with, especially in multigenerational environments where messaging that draws from residual taxonomies will likely be prevalent in the broader context. We often remind youth (and adults) that we can deeply care for one another and worship together and see facets of life differently, including our understanding of taxonomies in sexuality. At the same time, we recognize youth will not connect with everyone in the broader community and need not aim to do so.

We can also help youth understand the usefulness of taxonomies that may be more familiar to other church members without feeling unsettled by perspectives and feedback that may challenge their own taxonomy. Even giving the youth language around residual, dominant, and emerging taxonomies can be helpful in locating the broader culture and the local church context in order to more fully understand the clashes that can arise. We can also use the framing of translation between languages to help teens consider ways to be nimble with language in contexts where emerging frameworks are less familiar (i.e., a teen using descriptive language like "attracted to men/women/both" when speaking with an older adult in the church who may have a hard time understanding language such as "bicurious"). This moves the discussion outside of culture war rhetoric.

Just as we are equipping teens to engage their church, we want to better equip the church community. When the local church context is lacking in its ability to adequately engage in sexuality conversations, we want to create better churchwide environments so that the burden of navigating difficult spaces doesn't fall exclusively on the teens. This could involve purchasing and keeping resources at a church library or on shelves in meeting rooms that cover sexuality topics in meaningful ways. Resources could be available to staff and members to check out so they can have access to resourcing at the local church that is faith-congruent and nuanced. We can elevate the voices of sexual minority individuals who are members of the faith community by sharing their stories insofar as they would like in either private or public forums. We can also consider bringing in speakers who can offer talks to parents/staff about human sexuality in order to better equip the local community. We can purchase video content to be available to staff that increases their effectiveness in working with teens navigating emerging sexual identities.

In addition to cultivating relationships with youth and helping them understand the broader church context, there is value in buffering against some of the harm that can happen in church contexts. Youth will benefit from youth leaders checking in about certain conversations that may occur between youth in that context and being able to offer support if a teen is having a difficult time processing certain subjects, specifically those related to sexuality. When sermons (or guest lectures) at the church address sexuality, it will also help to make space for youth to process these with a youth leader or parent.

Peer Relationships

Finally, making it a priority to know a teen's community and peers, even non-Christian ones, will be of immense value in discipleship. If teens feel like certain conversations (including family challenges and sexuality milestone events), certain people (like nonbelieving peers or significant others), or certain terminologies (dominant or emergent taxonomies) are unwelcome, we miss an opportunity to speak into these aspects of life. Especially as teens are increasingly in peer groups that are adopting emergent sexual identity labels, we want to facilitate meaningful conversations with these youth (and their peers). We can't do so if we don't know about and invite conversation around these topics.

One concern that some Christian families (and ministers) have is that youth are being pushed into labels through peers and the cultural climate. While we currently steer away from "social contagion" language, we recognize that peers impact one another in countless ways, including the language and categories they draw from. We can imagine youth ministers introducing the idea of the looping effect to teens who are interested in thinking more about how culture informs their own sense of identity, behavior, and relationships. Rather than focusing on how the teen across from you is impacted by the looping effect, you could offer an opportunity to engage with how they see the looping effect at play in how teens think of themselves more broadly (in their school, in youth group, online, etc.). This allows teens to build the muscle of reflection on culture as they consider building meaningful friendships. It also allows them to consider the ways they themselves are impacted by sociocultural messaging (from the mental health field, peers, social media, and broader media portrayals) about sexuality.

When we consider sociocultural messaging, we are thinking beyond emerging categories and terminology. We are thinking of messaging around sexual behavior, spirituality, and fundamental beliefs about the meaning of life. Rather than either capitulating to aspects of cultural messaging that are at odds with Christian beliefs (e.g., the cultural message that sex is casual and not preserved for marriage or the message that the material world is all there is) or being a cultural warrior who may aim to alienate youth from peers who might be drawn to such messaging, we can help form youth to engage culture as cultural ambassadors. We can encourage teens to consider seeing their friendships as ways to share their faith and edify the faith of those around them, since many teens might not be currently thinking of their friendships in this way. Rather than acting on fear and attempting to box out peers who are non-Christian, we can encourage youth to both identify and build solid friendships with those who share their Christian convictions while also encouraging them to consider ways to encounter those who see things differently.

Cocreate a Ministry Climate That Is Emotionally and Spiritually Secure

When we speak of a ministry setting being emotionally and spiritually secure, we think of the security described in Scripture time and time again. This is the security that flows from unity with Christ—protection from spiritual death. We see in the witness of Christ that people who were alienated from society found a haven with Christ. Despite him saying those who would follow him would have nowhere to lay their head, we see the disciple John able to rest his head on Christ (John 13:23), even on the brink of Christ's Passion. This may be an image of security to draw from in our ministry. Even in the midst of pain, suffering, questions, doubts, and unknowns, we want youth to be able to rest beside Christ and within his body, the church.

What specifically do emotionally and spiritually secure ministry environments look like for sexual minority young people? We believe these environments will do the following:

- Foster appropriate and gradual emotional vulnerability, with boundaries.
- Support people in navigating stressors, including but not exclusively sexuality-related stressors.
- Include deep relational connections rooted in love, not fear, even when fears and disagreements may be present.
- Offer varied pathways for youth to imagine a future beyond marriage.

Some people will call this environment emotionally and spiritually "safe" rather than "secure"—a term that some readers may prefer to use. For other readers, the idea of "safety" will be off-putting. This kind of language has at times been used to insinuate that you can establish an environment free from pain, disagreement, challenges, or having to engage with discomfort. This has felt to some Christians like they cannot even teach Christian doctrine on sexuality or gender. And sometimes in current cultural contexts, "unsafe" is used as a catchall term to shut down further engagement during interactions that are tense or to alienate certain interlocutors from environments where people have differing opinions about sexuality. We are not suggesting that safety, or security for that matter, merely means that a person is in agreement with another about theological or philosophical assumptions or that a person will not encounter those who challenge them to think deeply and richly about faith. We find that these notions oversimplify the type of safety and security needed for growth, connection, and meaning.

Foster Emotional Vulnerability with Boundaries

Familial, mentoring, pastoral, and peer relationships hinge on establishing a place where youth have permission to be vulnerable. Vulnerability is fostered through gradual trust, time, and experiences that warrant a higher level of confidence for disclosure. We can teach teens that they are free to share gradually about their lives—including their sexual desires or lack thereof—with appropriate people but that no one has a right to know all aspects of our experience simply by knowing us. This can remind teens of the sacredness of their stories, an idea often lost in a label-focused culture, and bolster their ability to be gatekeepers of information that could be misused.

We also want to ensure that youth are not forced to be vulnerable or manipulated into vulnerability. This is one reason we strongly discourage people in ministry from disclosing vulnerable information about a young person without their permission and presence. Of course, specific safety concerns like suicidality and self-harm are exceptions to this rule; but in general, we want to show our youth that not everyone needs access to every part of their lives, and we do this best when we model it for them by respecting their privacy. Sometimes, youth contexts can become places where teens unload immensely vulnerable content without being taught how to appropriately gauge trust and security in the relationships there. We want to be good stewards of the time with youth by coaching them on how to confide in trustworthy supports without overdisclosing to everyone intimate details of their lives, including their sexuality.

A spiritually and emotionally secure environment is one in which people are able to set boundaries with one another. This means modeling boundaries for teens and then coaching and reminding them about how to set their own boundaries. For instance, if a teen is having an intense emotional experience on a youth trip after disclosing that they identify as asexual, other teens or adults will probably ask that teen what's going on. We want teens to know that they do not need to share everything with everyone; they can take time for self-reflection, reflection through journaling or prayer, or conversation with a support person without needing to be the focus of several peers' and adults' attention.

One of the boundaries that might come up related to emerging sexual identities is conversations around a person's sexual orientation, history, or behaviors. Depending on teens' cultural context, they may be in the habit of asking openly about one another's orientation/sexual history/behaviors. While sharing with peers may have value in specific relationships, some teens have shared with us that they feel greater pressure to land on an identity label for themselves when sexuality is a common topic of conversation. The teenage years are a valuable time to learn that, while vulnerability is important, we shouldn't share the same level of vulnerability with everyone.

Here's an example of how we might frame a conversation about the youth-group culture when conversations around sexual identity labels arise:

> In our youth group, we love that people can be open about so many things, including sexual attractions and orientation. We also want to remind you that each person is on their own journey with this, and sometimes questions like "Are you queer?" can put someone on the spot who isn't ready to share. We want to normalize that with questions people bring to you about your sexual identity, and any question that you don't feel comfortable responding to, you can simply say, "That's something I don't feel comfortable going into

right now." When trust is built, of course there is value in sharing about your sexual identity with others who can support you as you navigate it. This is true here in our youth group and also at school and in your friendships.

We can extrapolate the principles in this script to conversations around sexual behavior and sexual history as well. We want youth to feel secure to share their experiences with trusted others while recognizing that aspects of their sexuality are sacred and worth honoring by disclosing them with people who have shown themselves able to receive such information with reverence.

Support People in Navigating Stressors

An environment of emotional and spiritual security provides support as people manage their stressors. Many of today's youth experience similar stressors regardless of their experience of sexual attraction. It's worth remembering that, in ministering to the person, we are accounting for how often sexual minority youth are navigating life stressors, mood symptoms, familial challenges, peer conflicts, academic difficulties, and so on. We do want to attend to the overall well-being of these teens, reflecting ways in which they are doing well or struggling and connecting them to appropriate resources to cope with challenges that arise.

Another way youth environments can help with managing life stressors is simply giving a reprieve from them. Queer-identified youth have shared multiple times how attending youth retreats or events has felt like a "saving grace" that disrupts emotional distress. Getting to go to an event where youth can be a teen and act goofy and carefree is a needed break from the increasing stressors on young people. Continuing to offer access points for reprieve is no small thing. However, a few stressors appear uniquely or more frequently among sexual minority youth, including those drawn to emergent sexual identity categories.

One of these common stressors, which we've already discussed, is disclosure with loved ones (e.g., "How do I tell someone, whom do I tell, and when?"). Another is the considerations of labeling (e.g., "How do I identify privately and publicly?"). Another would be future-oriented questions (e.g., "Is it possible for me to be married heterosexually and have children? If I remain single, who will my community be?").

Another common stressor for sexual minority youth is being in spaces divided by sex. It would be very common in youth contexts for conversations about sexuality, pornography, masturbation, and attraction to be split in this way. It's important to consider how these spaces impact those who are attracted to the same sex. Part of the rationale for separating groups by sex when speaking of sexuality is to reduce discomfort in talking with the sex you are attracted to. This assumes heterosexuality in the youth. For a sexual minority youth, same-gender conversations can bring up alienation if the facilitator assumes that everyone's attraction is to the opposite sex.

Another facet of splitting by sex can involve sleeping arrangements, which can bring up occasions for sexual temptation, especially if youth are sharing beds with other youth of the same sex. It is essential to acknowledge that, in the same way that heterosexual youth are not attracted to every person of the opposite sex, sexual minority youth aren't attracted to every person of the same sex. And yet, there are times where sexual minority youth have shared about the stress of being in same-sex environments where discretion (around changing clothes, for instance) can be forgotten because of the assumption of heterosexuality.

Now, we aren't implying that every youth environment ought to do away with any and all opportunities for divisions by sex. Peer affiliation among same-sex peers can be valuable in facilitating a sense of belonging and connection. When it comes to the consideration of breaking up groups by sex, it is worth reflecting on the necessity or purpose behind frequent divisions of this kind, especially in the current landscape. Do we separate based on sex because doing so has clear value and utility? Do we do it to avoid distractions? Do we care about the fact that youth attracted to people of the same sex have been disproportionately unprotected by this approach?

Instead of entirely eliminating gender-specific groups, we have found it helpful to preserve these groups at times while also mixing in other group options not tied to gender. At a time when gender is already such a point of focus, dividing groups in different ways decentralizes gender. It also helps teens cultivate friendship and healthy opportunities for gradual vulnerability across differences, including sex differences—a skill that will benefit their future adult relationships as well as their current relationships.

Regarding sleeping arrangements, we recommend you offer guidance for how to navigate these experiences as a community and support one another. One aspect of this is encouraging standards of discretion and privacy with regard to changing and attire for sleeping. This can help reduce additional stressors for some sexual minority youth. Another aspect of this is inviting youth to consider whether a sleeping arrangement is going to be difficult for them (e.g., because of unkind behavior of youth in their room or because a crush is assigned to the same room). We want to encourage youth to talk to a youth leader if this is the case to make an alternative arrangement.

Include Connections Rooted in Love, Not Fear

An emotionally and spiritually secure environment is a place where people can move beyond fear-based relating to love-rooted connection.

Love-rooted connection can be thought of as connection that wills the good of the other for their own sake.[5] By this we mean that love goes beyond a desire for another person to merely experience subjective happiness. Love-rooted connection means wanting heaven for that person and seeing the role you play in that person's life as a support in helping that person know God, the supreme Good.

You may be wondering what this love-rooted connection involves in practice. It involves seeing the capacity of the youth for love, joy, and peace and helping them cultivate those through a relationship with God. It involves a willingness to suffer with youth and for them, praying for them, advocating for their tangible needs, and offering your presence in particular moments of pain. It involves celebrating the teen's strengths and talents, showing up at events, and listening to them as they share about their passions and dreams. It means believing your sexual minority youth can have a life of meaning, purpose, and obedience to God. It means elucidating the particular giftings that are uniquely present in each person and edifying your youth in repenting of sin and drawing near to God in areas of weakness.

Connection can go awry because of fear-based relating. Fear-based relating clouds our ability to see the other and will their good because of a reactivity in us. Fears could include fear of someone's salvation being in question, fear of bullying if a person experiences gender nonconformity, fear of a person being alienated for a minority experience, fear of our own association with a marginalized group, and so on. Fear-based relating can lead to overt or covert hatred, disgust, and conflict and can seek to alienate those whom you might see as different or other.

This fear-based relating can come out sideways in the language we are using or allowing to be used. Fear-based relating can involve stereotyping or making disparaging jokes at the expense of sexual minorities. This may surprise some readers. After all, how is it that fear can lead to stereotyping or making jokes at another's expense? Sometimes we see people make jokes to distance themselves from an experience they don't understand or that they feel overwhelmed by. Others make jokes or stereotype in denial of their own experience of sexuality that is difficult to acknowledge. Still others may make these comments to disassociate with private experiences they inaccurately associate with political or philosophical perspectives they disagree with. If we allow for unkind comments about sexual minorities, the effectiveness and credibility of our Christian ministry is undermined. More often than not, the enabling of these comments comes not from saying them but from remaining silent when they are said.

While we often think of fear-based relating from youth leaders and parents, it can also happen among youth themselves. When fear-based reactions occur among youth, youth ministers and other trusted adults can respond with questions that help people identify the source of the fears or anxieties and reduce those fears or anxieties. This means helping teens who are reactive to sexual minority peers process their fears and other reactions rather than enabling behaviors that isolate youth who are sexual minorities. This also means helping teens who have a hard time seeing any Christian with a traditional sexual ethic as anything other than bigoted by encouraging them to encounter those who hold such convictions with respect, care, and humility and to learn more about them over time.

Mocking comments toward sexual minority youth are often made by their peers rather than by adults. This means that youth mentors and pastors will benefit from learning how to respond to these comments without shaming the speaker. Sometimes, this is best done privately, but other times it will be important to address this publicly so as not to turn a blind eye to comments or lead youth to believe such behavior is acceptable in Christian settings. To discern which circumstance is which, it's worth asking the following questions:

1. Is this the first time this has occurred, in which case I can speak one-on-one with someone and give them an opportunity to address the comment publicly later with the group and apologize?

2. Is this an ongoing pattern, even with redirection, in which such comments could be impacting the overall culture without public acknowledgment and redirection?
3. Is the youth who is making the comment able to receive feedback?
4. If I say nothing, will other youth believe that I agree with the comment made or that the community more broadly does?

Here are a few ways to respond (privately and/or publicly) to disparaging comments from youth without shaming them:

> I want to remind us all that we don't talk about people like that here. As Christians, we want to honor the dignity of people, without exception.

> Perhaps you have concerns about people you may disagree with around sexuality. If so, I'd love to discuss them with you. But calling people names when we disagree with them isn't a way to help bring the gospel to others. We want to find ways to respectfully engage with people we don't see eye to eye with. If you're having a hard time understanding and seeing someone as a person made in God's image, that's an opportunity to invite Christ in to help transform your way of seeing others. The more we can conform our way of seeing to Christ's, the closer we draw to his heart. Further, we can come to see his sacred image in the person we previously struggled to know. God is prepared to bless us as we get to know people we previously might have diminished or rejected. He has so much to teach us through the people he brings into our lives.

> How might it feel if you heard someone talk that way about you? What if we had youth here who identify that way—would they feel loved by Christ hearing us talk that way?

> For a larger youth ministry: I know you might be thinking that no one here has a sexual minority experience, but there are people in

our community who are navigating sexuality and faith questions. We want to talk in a way that remembers they're here and communicates that we're glad they are part of our community.

Offer Varied Pathways

Another way to craft an emotionally and spiritually secure ministry environment is to be careful about how we portray what a fulfilled life looks like. Some ministries have overemphasized family-centered images to the exclusion of other possible meaningful life trajectories. Too often, youth get the sense that the only path forward for their life is marriage and a nuclear family. This pattern is especially salient in Western societies and church communities, which are oriented around marriage and the nuclear family in profound ways.

If teens are simply being told that the only path of fulfillment for them is marriage, what does this mean for youth drawn to emerging categories like "asexual" and "aromantic"? What is their trajectory within our communities? How about for the teen who is experiencing exclusively same-sex attraction?

While we don't want to negate the beauty of marriage as the common calling for most people, we also want to recognize the place of singleness and the rich history of Christians remaining unmarried. After all, the perfect man, Jesus himself, did not marry. His familial ties were expanded to those who do his will, as recorded in Matthew 12:50: "For whoever does the will of my Father in heaven is my brother and sister and mother." Many who followed after him remained permanently unmarried as a way to single-heartedly serve God. Even now, there are many in our churches who are seeking to follow Christ and are not called into marriage. We do well to introduce our youth to models who are living singleness with grace and peace in the midst of its challenges, much in the same way we do well to elevate married couples who model healthy and happy family life to our youth.

Given that young people are on average getting married later in life, and more people than ever before are not getting married, it is increasingly important to make space for singleness as a pathway for virtue and meaning in life. In the same way that a youth group may invite a married couple, a clergyperson, or a missionary to give a talk to youth, teens will also benefit from hearing the stories of single people, including single sexual minorities, seeking God in their lives.

Offer Discipleship

When thinking about future-oriented discernment, we find ourselves in the realm of ongoing discipleship. It's essential to take a long-term view, as oftentimes we as ministers/leaders will see only one fraction of a youth's larger spiritual journey. We believe that discipleship must be *offered* rather than imposed on someone or held out as an expectation. This is how Jesus treats us in our own walks with him. He honors our freedom while knocking at the door and inviting us into deeper relationship with him.

Discipleship means fostering growth toward Christlikeness. Discipleship often takes the form of one-on-one relationships, small group discussion, Scripture reading, prayer, confession, corporate worship, and other spiritual practices. It entails teaching and modeling how to engage in common spiritual practices for the purpose of enhancing one's relationship with Christ and applying those practices to the particular life of each person.

Discipleship has direction and is oriented toward a *telos*—that is, a goal or end. It is not relational merely for the sake of maintaining relationship. When it comes to the realm of youth sexuality, we recommend framing discipleship through the lens of stewardship. That is, we want to help a young person reflect on ways to be a good steward of their life, including their sexuality.

We want to turn now to two important aspects of discipleship within emerging sexual identities. We want to offer a framework for discipleship that involves sexual stewardship and prepare you to engage relationally around queer theory. Let's turn to this now.

Discipling Toward Sexual Stewardship

We want to close out our ministry recommendations with a reflection on sexual stewardship. In the same way we might discuss stewardship in the realm of finances or relationships, we want to talk about stewarding our sexuality as a pathway to freedom and authentic living.

Conversations with youth about stewardship need to apply to the unique experiences of youth drawn to emergent categories. You may be wondering, "How could you communicate this idea of stewardship to a youth who identifies with an emergent sexual identity label?" Let's take the example of a youth who is longing to know what sexual stewardship means in the context of being a bicurious youth. Here's what a minister could say in this situation:

> It's normal to be curious about your desires, what they mean, and where they will take you. God delights in you any time you want to share anything about your experience with him, including your sexual/romantic desires or crushes. He is not disgusted and is eager to be close to you in this.
>
> Our culture sometimes invites people to explore their sexuality through sexual behaviors to see what fits. The culture's focus is on authenticity; we're told to look inward to know how we ought to express our sexuality.
>
> As Christians, we don't believe that looking inward is an end in itself or a reliable pathway to authenticity. Rather, our focus is on bringing all of our experiences, desires, crushes, and longings to Jesus and seeking to follow his commands within our relationships.

We want to clarify what God is asking of us, learning with his help to treat ourselves and those in our lives in ways that honor our dignity and his plan. This is the path of authenticity and true freedom.

Sexual stewardship isn't merely about changing behavior or using or avoiding certain language. (Similarly, financial stewardship isn't merely about saving money, donating to charities, or avoiding irresponsible spending.) It's about cultivating a way of seeing and relating to ourselves and others that honors our dignity and reflects what we are made for. Sexual stewardship is about understanding our very sexuality as a gift to be cultivated for the glory of God.

Even though we are not all called into relationships that are sexual, we are all sexual beings who can submit our desires to Christ. This means we will be called to sacrifices in different moments and in different ways. Ultimately, to whatever extent our sexual desires are unfulfilled in this lifetime, they point us to what we are made for, which is perfect unity with God in heaven.

All of us are called to make our life a gift to God and others. This doesn't necessarily involve sexual activity, but it means being connected to our desires and longings, our passions and dreams, trusting that God will lead us as we surrender our bodies in service of him.

For those of us who are single, giving our bodies to God involves seeking to abstain from sexual activity. That's the "no" in our stewardship. That may sound boring and depressing, but actually, amazing Christians throughout history have made a gift of their bodies and lives *because of* their singleness. Some sexual minorities feel particularly convinced that singleness is for them due to the direction of their attraction (or lack of sexual attraction). Single-heartedness for the Lord as a single person comes with its own challenges and its own gifts. Singleness is best navigated when we experience belonging in a community of believers who are also invested in supporting this call.

For those of us who are married, stewardship means saying no to romantic interests, crushes (which will happen), and sexual activity outside of our spouse. That may feel restrictive in some ways, and it is. Authentic freedom always involves a no to something. (For example, saying yes to the freedom to drive a car means saying no to breaking the rules of the road.) Marriage is a beautiful calling. It invites us into a relationship with another person that reflects the unity of God with us, his faithfulness to us, and our response to him. Even those of us who aren't married can learn from the beautiful self-giving love of a married couple. Marriage, like singleness, is cultivated in the context of a Christian community that supports the mission of each individual family.

We can see in the above script an emphasis on both what Christians say no to in stewardship and what we say yes to. After all, we follow a form of life that involves transformation of our values, behaviors, language, and so much in between. We don't shy away from the reality that a Christian vision for sexual ethics is distinct from the visions communicated by our surrounding cultures.

Relationally Engaging with Queer Theory

In sexuality conversations around emergent categories, we have seen many ministers emphasize disputation strategies over relationship building with adolescents, focusing on winning an argument instead of attuning to the person across from them and thinking through their questions with them. If you dig in and tell them that they are wrong, do you think they will just thank you and walk away satisfied that you put them on the right path? More likely than not, they will harbor objections to your dismissal of their ideas and turn away from you as a resource in their journey.

If we avoid engaging with youth as if they are political activists, we remain open to the things they are considering and refrain from simply debating queer theory with every youth navigating emerging identity labels. Not all youth will benefit from conversations about queer theory. But some youth may benefit from us exploring the degree to which they are being informed by queer theory or the looping effect in their own sexuality journey. We turn now to thinking through how to engage with this in ministry.

Insofar as a teen is actively engaging with queer theory or wanting to discuss broader cultural narratives, we recommend you demonstrate *genuine* curiosity about the theory or idea. But what does curiosity actually look and sound like?

- Ask the youth in front of you more questions about the theories they are drawing upon. These should be genuine questions of interest to you rather than a technique that could be experienced as manipulative to the adolescent.
- Reflect back what you hear so that they (and you) know you are following along with their thought process.
- In addition to questions about the theory as they understand it, ask them good questions about how they understand the assertions that come from queer theory. Does queer theory align with a Christian vision of the world, and if so, to what extent?
- Wonder with them what queer theory has to offer or contributes of value, from their perspective. Ask them what points within queer theory feel incomplete or they have questions about. Offer critical reflections on queer theory *with* youth, not *at* them.
- Invite the teen to share how they process your reflections. Invite them to continue to "wrestle with God" as they engage with queer theory for themself.

Slow down when you feel tempted to craft your argument against aspects of queer theory that depart from a robust understanding of the human person. Ask more questions. Be present. Be genuinely curious, and realize that the person in front of you believes they have found something worthwhile in a meaning-making structure that you disagree with. So, try to understand what is compelling to them about the theory they are holding on to. Curiosity builds relationships. It does not cut ties or dismiss the person or their ideas.

Conversely, refrain from simply being a passive observer of your youth as they engage with queer theory. Give them the opportunity to understand a Christian framework.[6] Acknowledge with them that cultural norms at any period of history fail to account for the robustness of God's vision of the human person. Consider together any missing pieces in queer theory, as we have mapped out earlier in this book. Do so with an open hand, not because you don't firmly believe what you are sharing but because an invitational approach to the gospel allows our youth to honor their freedom while trusting their ability to step into the life of faith more deeply over time.

It's worth noting that not every sexual minority youth is drawn to queer theory, per se. In fact, we are seeing that some youth (including sexual and gender minorities) are absolutely unaware of queer theory as such, and some who are aware are frustrated by some of its more extreme aspects. We want to shape these young people in modeling thoughtful and respectful debate rather than encouraging volatility and mockery of these positions.

Discipleship, illustrated in this way, is meant to intentionally cultivate a young person's walk with Christ and connect them to the broader community of the church. Discipleship allows us to see in ourselves and in the lives of those we accompany the saving power of Christ at work. Discipleship points to particular ends. At its best, discipleship allows us to accompany young people where they find themselves, inviting them to become the cultural ambassadors our communities desperately need. Discipleship in this context requires some creativity and a great deal of patience. Most of all, it brings us into a deeper realization of our need for God, for whom nothing is impossible (Luke 1:37).

Discipleship moves the conversation about sexuality away from debates over causal pathways and essentialism versus constructivism. It allows us to recognize with a teen that, regardless of how they came to the place of experiencing what they experience, and describing their sexuality in the words that they do, they are invited into a creative space with God to explore his particular plan for their life. This is a plan that God will cocreate with us rather than one that he places on us as a heavy burden.

Bridging the Language Barrier

In many churches and many Christian homes, there is a language barrier today even with dominant terminology such as "gay" and "transgender." That barrier may seem even more challenging as we have introduced emerging sexual identities and microminoritized language for communicating sexual and gender identity at a more granular level. We want to offer a few suggestions for bridging the language barrier in ministry or parenting.

First, it is good to just be aware of changing language. Maybe you are just catching up with dominant taxonomies and are able to distinguish between sexual and gender identities. Maybe you have become familiar with the distinction between "transgender" and "nonbinary," and now we are telling you that may be dominant language, but it is not emergent. Now you can locate terms rather than simply be confused by them. The use of emerging terms may now become a source of information for how you relate to youth in ministry and parenting.

Second, listen carefully to young people. Listen respectfully and attentively. You are not compromising or making concessions by listening well to youth. They are reflecting a different culture and elements of another form of life—and perhaps they have one foot in that form of life and one foot in the form of life meant to be shaped by and lived out in the church. Think of conversations and check-ins as opportunities to establish and build trust, provide emotional support, improve communication, and foster self-confidence.

Third, identify the taxonomy. As you listen to a young person, what language is being used: Dominant? Emergent? Is there any reference to residual taxonomies? In your ministry setting or in your home, what language is most often used? How does that language shape expectations and behaviors? What language is being used by those you minister to? Do they shift language or filter in your presence? Keep in mind that they encounter the language either way, so filtering is a possibility as they weigh whether to open up about the language they are considering.

Fourth, try to understand how language functions for those you minister to or parent. Are they using this language to identify with nonnormative sexual or gender identities or for other reasons? Is this for self-exploration? Is this for belonging and community? Is this helping them navigate social relationships or expectations? Is this meant to reflect empowerment and autonomy?

Fifth, build genuine connections and trust through sustained relationships. Ask about the full scope of their life and interests. This means showing up for them and for those they care about by being physically present and emotionally available. Genuine connections increase emotional security and openness in relationships. These connections give them access to guidance (if and when they are open to it) and mentoring. They provide young people with long-term stability as they are able to count on you.

Finally, be respectful of what is "above the surface" (language and identity labels, microminoritized identity language) and focus on ministry that is "below the surface" (their heart and relationship with God). Remember that getting categories and terminology "right" is not ministry, although changes in language may result from ministry. Instead, support holistic development, affirm their worth, build resilience, encourage spiritual depth, and offer discipleship. Their more substantive questions have to do with how God sees them, whether they can trust in God as a good and loving Father, and whether they can trust God with their sexuality or gender. If you are weighing whether to speak into identity language (provide observations, share concerns, etc.), consider your relationship to them, the timing of when you might say something, and how it will be received.

Concluding Thoughts

As we bring our reflections to a close, we are reminded of countless adults who have shared that when they were teens, they needed a positive vision for their life as a Christian. Sexual minority youth are no exception to this rule. They need a form of life that makes sense to them, that gives them a sense of culture, purpose, and meaning.

This form of life includes a positive vision of sexuality, but it is also expansive enough to help foster spiritual maturity in many other aspects of life. Sexual minority youth need help seeing themselves more holistically and understanding how to relate to parents, faith community members, and peers who may be impacted by the looping effect.

They also need safe havens from the pressures of daily life, places to explore their spiritual questions alongside their sexuality questions. All teens will benefit from understanding the call God has placed on their lives in the realm of sexual stewardship. Teens who may be familiar with queer theory and interested in thinking it through will benefit from engaging with queer theory. Most of all, they need to be invited into a relationship with Jesus, who is seeking after them with the radical and unique love of a Father.

EPILOGUE

We hope that you are beginning to see a path forward in the complicated terrain of emerging sexual identities. We're sure we've left you with some unanswered questions, but we hope we've also offered you some better questions, and some answers to those questions, along the way.

We also anticipate that you have been able to get your bearings as you identify the historical factors that have made ministry around sexuality and faith less effective in our communities. You have greater insight into the controversies in care that have focused on change of orientation, identity, and/or behavior, and how you might begin to offer a more comprehensive approach to youth. You also now have a clearer sense of the various taxonomies available to young people and the ways in which ministry out of residual taxonomies presents challenges within a generation widely adopting emergent taxonomies. In doing so, we want to help you pave a way through the current age within which we are called to care.

As Christians who hope to serve as cultural ambassadors, we find comfort in the same encouragement we have shared with many sexual minorities and their families over the years: God is not surprised by where we are. He sees all of it, and more importantly, he sees each of us. He knows the intricacies of our stories, our hopes, our longings, and our fears. He sees the young people entrusted to our care and knows what each one needs.

Ministry can feel futile, exhausting, and disorienting at this time in history, when residual categories have fallen out of favor and dominant categories are being surpassed by emergent ones. And yet, it is here that Christ calls us to minister. We can think of no better path forward than to ask for his help and to trust in his provision. May we all continue to do so as we navigate this important ministry terrain.

ACKNOWLEDGMENTS

I, Mark, would like to thank Julia for her ongoing collaboration in the areas of sexual and gender identity. This is our third book together, and having Julia as a colleague to think through these challenging questions has been rewarding. Thank you for your dedication in tackling challenging topics together. It has been incredibly rewarding to work alongside you.

I am also grateful for my colleagues at Wheaton College and students and staff at the Sexual and Gender Identity (SGI) Institute, including David O'Connor (who assisted with the index for this book), Anna Brose, Mia Menassa, Ruth Fu, Carly Quibodeaux, Ian Sneller, Hannah Hawkins, Eli Matthews, Ruth Hueber, Will Motzel, Sarah Taetzsch, and administrative coordinator Jordan Anton. I am also grateful for my monthly case discussion group (Dr. Heather Brooke-Ryan, Dr. Emma Bucher, Dr. Charity Lane, Courtney Hanks, Ana Barend, and Dr. Elisabeth Wilson) and the fellows of SGI (in addition to Julia Sadusky: Dr. Janet Dean, Dr. Stephen Stratton, and Dr. Olya Zaporozhets).

I, Julia, would like to express gratitude to Mark for the ways he has modeled convicted civility, grace, and perseverance in his career as a psychologist specializing in sexuality and gender. Mostly, I am grateful for his spiritual maturity and commitment to Christ.

I could not and would not be where I am without your mentoring, friendship, and encouragement at many critical stages of my formation as a psychologist. It's been fun to watch each book "write itself," as the kids say.

I am also grateful for my family, dear friends, spiritual director, therapist, and colleagues, who have been an anchor for me throughout this project and beyond. In a particular way, I am dedicating this work to Lauren Tibbets and Johnny Sapienza. To Lauren—you are a light to me and so many, and doing life alongside you is one of God's greatest gifts to me. To Johnny—you took a risk in sharing your own journey of navigating sexuality and faith so many years ago during a Florida road trip. Your willingness to confide in me changed the trajectory of my life personally and professionally in ways I am eternally grateful for.

Collectively, we would like to thank Dr. Gregory Coles for his ongoing editing expertise and the entire team at Brazos Press for your willingness to support this project and help us bring it to its final form. We also would like to express our appreciation to Dr. Abigail Favale, Anna Carter, and Dr. Stephen Stratton for your thoughtful feedback as we developed this project.

We are also grateful for the many churches and ministries we have had the opportunity to work with over the years. As we've partnered with you in outward-facing presentations to your community, staff training, and pastoral equipping, you have sharpened us and helped us think through the practical applications of biblical theology and psychology.

Finally, we want to thank the countless clients who have trusted us with their stories at the intersection of sexual identity and faith. We are better Christian psychologists for knowing you and having the privilege of accompanying you.

NOTES

Chapter 1 A Culture of Sexual Identities

1. Rob Cover, *Emergent Identities: New Sexualities, Genders and Relationships in a Digital Age* (Routledge, 2019), 15, 25–28.
2. "National Survey on LGBTQ Youth Mental Health 2019," The Trevor Project, 2019, https://www.thetrevorproject.org/survey-2019.
3. Mark A. Yarhouse and Julia Sadusky, *Emerging Gender Identities: Understanding the Diverse Experiences of Today's Youth* (Brazos, 2022).
4. Mark A. Yarhouse, Janet Dean, Stephen P. Stratton, and Julia Sadusky, "Micro-Minoritized and Emerging Sexual and Gender Identities," symposium conducted at the Christian Association for Psychological Studies national conference, Atlanta, GA, March 22, 2024.
5. Raymond Williams, *Marxism and Literature* (Oxford University Press, 1977), 121–23.
6. Williams, *Marxism and Literature*, 122.
7. See Hanne Blank, *Straight: The Surprisingly Short History of Heterosexuality* (Beacon, 2012).
8. Cover, *Emergent Identities*, 19. Interestingly, the earliest conceptualizations of transgender experiences were conflated with homosexuality; transgender identities were seen as a subset of homosexual attraction.
9. We want to thank Dr. Abigail Favale for her reflections within this section, which added greater nuance to our discussion of residual categories.
10. Cover, *Emergent Identities*, 117, 119.
11. Williams, *Marxism and Literature*, 121.
12. E.g., a 2014 Gallup poll indicated that 42 percent of Americans say that a person is born gay, which was up from 13 percent in 1977. Justin McCarthy, "Americans' Views on Origins of Homosexuality Remain Split," Gallup, May 28, 2014, https://news.gallup.com/poll/170753/americans-views-origins-homosexuality-remain-split.aspx.
13. Cover, *Emergent Identities*, 114.

14. Cover, *Emergent Identities*, 119.
15. Adam B. Lerner, "The Supreme Court's Most Memorable Quotes on Gay Marriage," *Politico*, June 26, 2015, https://www.politico.com/story/2015/06/supreme-court-justices-opinions-memorable-quotes-gay-marriage-119477.
16. Lerner, "Supreme Court's Most Memorable Quotes."
17. Lisa M. Diamond, *Sexual Fluidity: Understanding Women's Love and Desire* (Harvard University Press, 2009), cited in Cover, *Emergent Identities*, 123.
18. Diamond, *Sexual Fluidity*.
19. Lisa Diamond, interview with Anne Strainchamps, "The New Science of Sexual Fluidity," To the Best of Our Knowledge, February 13, 2021, https://www.ttbook.org/interview/new-science-sexual-fluidity.
20. Lisa M. Diamond, "Sexual Fluidity in Male and Females," *Current Sexual Health Reports* 8 (2016): 249–56, https://psych.utah.edu/_resources/documents/people/diamond/Sexual%20Fluidity%20in%20Males%20and%20Females.pdf.
21. Williams, *Marxism and Literature*, 123.
22. Cover, *Emergent Identities*, 30.
23. Cover, *Emergent Identities*, 2.
24. Aki Gormezano, interview with Meghan McDonough, host, *Science Quickly*, podcast, "How to Explore Your Sexuality, According to Science," Scientific American, February 14, 2024, https://www.scientificamerican.com/podcast/episode/how-to-explore-your-sexuality-according-to-science. Thank you to Stephen P. Stratton for bringing this podcast to our attention.
25. Cover, *Emergent Identities*, 6.
26. Cover, *Emergent Identities*, 2.
27. Cover, *Emergent Identities*, 2.
28. Cover, *Emergent Identities*, 73.
29. Cover, *Emergent Identities*, 83.
30. Cover, *Emergent Identities*, 3.
31. Cover, *Emergent Identities*, 26.
32. Cover, *Emergent Identities*, 54–55.
33. Stacy T. Watnick, interview with Meghan McDonough, host, *Science Quickly*, podcast, "How to Explore Your Sexuality, According to Science," Scientific American, February 14, 2024, https://www.scientificamerican.com/podcast/episode/how-to-explore-your-sexuality-according-to-science.
34. Cover, *Emergent Identities*, 32–33, 38–41.
35. Readers familiar with Charles Taylor's *A Secular Age* will appreciate how the emergent in some ways reflects and extends the "expressive individualism" and search for "authenticity": "There arises in Western societies a generalized culture of 'authenticity,' or expressive individualism, in which people are encouraged to find their own way, discover their own fulfillment, 'do their own thing.' The ethic of authenticity originates in the Romantic period, but it has utterly penetrated popular culture only in recent decades." Taylor, *A Secular Age* (Harvard University Press, 2007), 299. An element of this expressive individualism and authenticity is the turning within for guidance on self and the curation of personhood and identity. Thank you to Stephen P. Stratton for helping us make this connection.
36. A related concern has to do with relational boundaries. Cover's observation is that the emergent sexual and gender identities lend themselves to the creation

of a new "sexual citizenship" with its own set of expectations and responsibilities, so that young people are able to "avoid slippage from, say, friendship into the sexual." Cover, *Emergent Identities*, 61.

37. "1% of the Population," Asexual, January 19, 2021, https://www.asexual.be/en/2021/01/1-van-de-bevolking.

38. "1.7% of Sexual Minority Adults Identify as Asexual," Williams Institute, August 8, 2019, https://williamsinstitute.law.ucla.edu/press/sm-asexuals-press-release.

39. "Asexual and Ace Spectrum Youth," The Trevor Project, October 26, 2020, https://www.thetrevorproject.org/research-briefs/asexual-and-ace-spectrum-youth.

40. "Asexual and Ace Spectrum Youth."

41. Ace Community Survey Team, "Ace Community Survey Summary Report," October 23, 2023, https://acecommunitysurvey.org/2023/10/23/2021-ace-community-survey-summary-report.

42. "General FAQ," Asexuality Visibility and Education Network, https://www.asexuality.org/?q=general.html.

43. Susan McQuillan, "The Many Shades of Asexuality: Graysexuality, Quoisexuality, Apothisexuality, and More," *Psychology Today*, January 15, 2024, https://www.psychologytoday.com/us/blog/cravings/202401/asexuality-demisexuality-graysexuality-and-more.

44. "Ace Women," The Ace and Aro Advocacy Project, March 26, 2022, https://taaap.org/2022/03/26/ace-women.

45. McQuillan, "Many Shades of Asexuality."

46. Daniel Copulsky and Phillip L. Hammack, "Asexuality, Graysexuality, and Demisexuality: Distinctions in Desire, Behavior, and Identity," *Journal of Sex Research* 60, no. 2 (2023): 221. See also Amy N. Antonsen et al., "Ace and Aro: Understanding Differences in Romantic Attractions Among Persons Identifying as Asexual," *Archives of Sexual Behavior* 49, no. 5 (2020): 1615–30; and Jessica J. Hille, "Beyond Sex: A Review of Recent Literature on Asexuality," *Current Opinion in Psychology* 49 (2023).

47. Ana C. Carvalho and David L. Rodrigues, "Sexuality, Sexual Behavior, and Relationships of Asexual Individuals: Differences Between Aromantic and Romantic Orientation," *Archives of Sexual Behavior* 51, no. 4 (2022): 2159.

48. Blank, *Straight*, xiv.

49. Brandon Ambrosino, "Invention of 'Heterosexuality,'" BBC, March 15, 2017, https://bbc.com/future/article/20170315-the-invention-of-heterosexuality.

50. Blank, *Straight*, 43.

51. Blank, *Straight*, 1–21.

52. Ambrosino, "Invention of 'Heterosexuality.'"

53. Blank, *Straight*, 16–17.

54. Neither conceptualization made any significant inroads in the penal code (Blank, *Straight*, 17–18). Variations on those codes were crafted when Germany united, and it was Adolf Hitler who tragically used the newer penal codes to kill many thousands of homosexuals. The law against such behavior was not removed until 1969.

55. James G. Kiernan, "Responsibility in Sexual Perversion," *Chicago Medical Recorder* 3 (May 1892): 185–210, cited in Jonathan Ned Katz, *Invention of Heterosexuality* (Dutton, 1995), 234.

56. Katz, *Invention of Heterosexuality*, 235.

57. For Christians, we might be inclined to think that "heterosexuality" as a term would map cleanly onto what we see in Scripture in male/female relationships, which form the basis for Christian marriage and reflect certain transcendent realities, such as the metaphorical relationship between husband/wife and God/humanity. Still, we do not need to hold "heterosexuality" or "heterosexual" as though the terms themselves came down from Mount Sinai. Rather, the terms themselves are socially constructed and can be used to normalize any and all sexual behaviors between a man and a woman, which would contrast a Christian understanding of sexual ethics. We can value the use of this language and simultaneously recognize that we hold language and taxonomies with some gentleness and humility. In this context, gentleness and humility will prepare us well for ministry to those who experience a nonnormative sexuality, identity, or orientation. This posture will also help us have more empathy for those who are drawn to emergent taxonomies and demonstrate more curiosity for how microminoritized identities function for young people.

58. It is interesting that most people in the BDSM/kink and CNM communities do not identify themselves as part of the LGBTQ+ community unless they are LGBTQ+ and have interest in BDSM, kink, or CNM, whereas many people who identify along the ace spectrum do identify with the LGBTQ+ community, either by virtue of their increased likelihood of having a diverse gender identity or simply because their sexual identity seems to reflect an LGBTQ+ posture.

59. Margaret Nichols and James P. Fedor, "Treating Sexual Problems in Clients Who Practice 'Kink,'" in *The Wiley Handbook of Sex Therapy*, ed. Zoë D. Peterson (Wiley & Sons, 2017), 426–27.

60. Angel Renee Kalafatis-Russell, "Doing Kink vs. Being Kinky: A Systematic Scoping Review of the Literature on BDSM Behavior, Orientation, and Identity" (master's thesis, University of North Florida, 2021).

61. One similarity between LGBTQ+ identities and other nonnormative sexualities like CNM and BDSM/kink is that they were once classified as mental disorders. Homosexuality was removed from the list of mental disorders in the 1970s, while paraphilias like BDSM were removed much more recently, with the 2013 publication of the *Diagnostic and Statistical Manual of Mental Disorders*, 5th edition (DSM-5), and reaffirmed in the text revision of the DSM (DSM-5-TR). In the DSM-5 and DSM-5-TR, we see a distinction between paraphilias and paraphilic disorders. While all atypical sexual interests (paraphilias) used to be considered mental health concerns (including various fetishes, sadism, masochism, and so on), today they are thought of as paraphilic disorders only *if they are distressing to the person or acting on the interest would entail harm to another.* While we have concerns about this conceptual shift, we want to focus our engagement here on whether declassification as a mental disorder indicates the emergence of a new sexual orientation.

62. Heide Busse et al., "Prevalence and Associated Harm of Engagement in Self-Asphyxial Behaviours ('Choking Game') in Young People: A Systematic

Review," *Archives of Disease in Childhood* 100, no. 12 (2015), https://pmc.ncbi.nlm.nih.gov/articles/PMC4680200.
   63. Cover, *Emergent Identities*, 5.
   64. Cover, *Emergent Identities*, 5.

Chapter 2 Queer Theory

1. For a more robust treatment of queer theory and how it contributes to shifts in Western thought on sexuality and gender, see Abigail Favale, *The Genesis of Gender: A Christian Theory* (Ignatius, 2022).
   2. According to David Halperin, "AIDS activism has had to challenge traditional modes of empowering knowledge as well as traditional modes of authorizing and legitimating power. It has had to find ways of breaking down monopolies of professional expertise, ways of democratizing knowledge, and ways of credentializing the disempowered so that they can intervene in the medical and governmental administration of the epidemic." Halperin, *Saint Foucault: Toward a Gay Hagiography* (Oxford University Press, 1995), 28.
   3. Teresa de Lauretis, "Queer Theory: Lesbian and Gay Sexualities: An Introduction," *differences* 3, no. 2 (Summer 1991): xvi.
   4. de Lauretis, "Queer Theory," v.
   5. de Lauretis, "Queer Theory," x.
   6. Halperin, *Saint Foucault*, 32.
   7. According to Judith Butler, the production and policing of norms can create violence toward those who experience nonnormative sexualities and genders (Daniel R. Patterson, *Reforming a Theology of Gender: Constructive Reflections on Judith Butler and Queer Theory* [Cascade Books, 2022], 95). Patterson observes, "In Butler's thinking, norms are *not* fundamentally problematic nor dispensable aspects of subjectivity, but are foundational and necessary, which means that norms imposed from the outside on people, while not necessarily violations, must always be susceptible to disabling. In this sense, the critique Butler's theory exacts does not *do away with* gender categories or norms, but opens up to perpetual re-evaluation and therefore recalibration, reconditioning, or *reform*" (101–2).
   8. Rob Cover, *Emergent Identities: New Sexualities, Genders and Relationships in a Digital Age* (Routledge, 2019), 111.
   9. Halperin, *Saint Foucault*, 32.
   10. Halperin, *Saint Foucault*, 33.
   11. Halperin, *Saint Foucault*, 44.
   12. Halperin, *Saint Foucault*, 44–46.
   13. Worldview integration is defined as "an attempt to reposition psychology with a cognitive frame that is coherently embedded within Christian thought and premised on Christian assumptions." William L. Hathaway and Mark A. Yarhouse, *The Integration of Psychology and Christianity: A Domain-Based Approach* (IVP Academic, 2021), 41.
   14. G. K. Chesterton, *G. K. Chesterton: The Autobiography of G. K. Chesterton* (Ignatius, 2006), 212.
   15. David A. C. Bennett, *Queering the Queer: An Exploration of How Gay Celibate Asceticism Can Renew and Inform the Role of Desire in Contemporary*

Anglican Theology (doctoral thesis, University of Oxford, 2022), 17. "Queerness is no longer seen as an enemy to clarity or [analytic theology's] values and ends, but part of the eyes of [analytic theology's] heart being opened and formed by Jesus Christ crucified, the very wisdom of God." Bennett, "Returning to Spiritual Sense: Cruciform Power and Queer Identities in Analytic Theology," *Religions* 14, no. 12 (2023): 1454.

16. Judith Butler, "Performative Acts and Gender Constitution: An Essay in Phenomenology and Feminist Theory," in *Performing Feminisms: Feminist Critical Theory and Theatre*, ed. Sue-Ellen Case (Johns Hopkins University Press, 1990), 527.

17. Butler, "Performative Acts and Gender Constitution," 522.

18. James K. A. Smith, *Imagining the Kingdom: How Worship Works* (Baker Academic, 2013).

19. Rob Cover, *Identity and Digital Communication: Concepts, Theories, Practices* (Routledge, 2023), 27.

20. Cover, *Identity and Digital Communication*, 38.

21. Cover, *Identity and Digital Communication*, 39.

22. Cover, *Identity and Digital Communication*, 39.

23. Cover, *Identity and Digital Communication*, 49.

24. Cover, *Emergent Identities*, 144.

25. Judith Butler, "Rethinking Vulnerability and Resistance," in *Vulnerability in Resistance*, ed. Judith Butler, Zeynep Gambetti, and Leticia Sabsay (Duke University Press, 2016), cited in Cover, *Emergent Identities*, 145.

26. Mark A. Yarhouse and Olya Zaporozhets, *Costly Obedience: What We Can Learn from the Celibate Gay Christian Community* (Zondervan, 2019), 207. "Charles" is a pseudonym for an interviewed participant in the study.

27. Yarhouse and Zaporozhets, *Costly Obedience*, 207–8.

28. Eve Kosofsky Sedgwick, *Epistemology of the Closet* (University of California Press, 1990), cited in Halperin, *Saint Foucault*, 34.

29. Halperin, *Saint Foucault*, 35.

30. Halperin, *Saint Foucault*, 35.

31. Marli Huijer, "A Critical Use of Foucault's Art of Living," *Foundations of Science* 22 (2017): 323.

32. Jay Emerson Johnson, *Peculiar Faith: Queer Theology for Christian Witness* (Seabury, 2014), 34.

33. J. Johnson, *Peculiar Faith*.

34. J. Johnson, *Peculiar Faith*, 22.

35. J. Johnson, *Peculiar Faith*, 26.

36. Linn Marie Tonstad, "Ambivalent Loves: Christian Theologies, Queer Theologies," *Literature and Theology* 31, no. 4 (2017): 473, 477.

37. J. Johnson, *Peculiar Faith*, 29.

38. J. Johnson, *Peculiar Faith*, 30.

39. J. Johnson, *Peculiar Faith*, 57.

40. J. Johnson, *Peculiar Faith*, 45.

41. J. Johnson, *Peculiar Faith*.

42. Justin Sabia-Tanis, "Holy Creation, Wholly Creative: God's Intention for Gender Diversity," in *Understanding Transgender Identities: Four Views*, ed.

James K. Beilby and Paul Rhodes Eddy (Baker Academic, 2019), 204. Similarly, Micah Melody Taberner describes gender transitioning as "co-creation in partnership with the Divine." Rather than emphasize the journey in this particular essay, she discusses the importance of naming throughout Scripture. See Taberner, "Transition as an Act of Co-Creation in Partnership with the Divine: A Reflection," Pacific School of Religion, June 6, 2023, https://www.psr.edu/news/transition-as-an-act-of-co-creation-in-partnership-with-the-divine-a-reflection-by-micah-melody-taberner. Although we appreciate the significance of naming in relation to transitioning, we see managing dysphoria as the more salient consideration, particularly in terms of medical necessity.

43. J. Johnson, *Peculiar Faith*.

44. Thank you to Abigail Favale for her reflections on queer theory that bolstered this section of the book.

Chapter 3 How Sexual Identities Come into Being

1. Ian Hacking, "Making Up People," *London Review of Books* 28, no. 16 (2006): 23–26.

2. N. Haslam, "Looping Effects and the Expanding Concept of Mental Disorder," *Journal of Psychopathology* 22, no. 4 (2016): 4–9.

3. Ian Hacking, "Making Up People," in *Reconstructing Individualism: Autonomy, Individuality, and the Self in Western Thought*, ed. Thomas C. Heller, Morton Sosna, and David E. Wellbery (Stanford University Press, 1986), 222–36. Given our previous chapter on queer theory and Michel Foucault, it may be noteworthy that Hacking traces the concern with labeling and naming to Foucault, who writes, "We should try to discover how it is that subjects are gradually, progressively, really and materially constituted through a multiplicity of organisms, forces, energies, and materials, desires, thoughts, etc." Michel Foucault, "Two Lectures," in *Power/Knowledge: Selected Interviews and Other Writings, 1972–1977*, ed. Colin Gordon, trans. Kate Soper (Pantheon, 1980), 97, cited in Hacking, "Making Up People," in *Reconstructing Individualism*, 226. Hacking considers whether the more recent attempts at making people up are "linked to control" and reflect "a particular medico-forensic-political language of individual and social control." Hacking, "Making Up People," in *Reconstructing Individualism*, 226.

4. Ian Hacking, "The Looping Effects of Human Kinds," in *Causal Cognition: An Interdisciplinary Approach*, ed. Dan Sperber et al. (Oxford University Press, 1995), 368.

5. Hacking, "Looping Effects of Human Kinds," 370.

6. Ian Hacking, "How 'Natural' Are 'Kinds' of Sexual Orientation?," *Law and Philosophy* 12, no. 1 (2002): 104.

7. "Events in life can now be seen as events of a new kind, a kind that may not have been conceptualized when the event was experienced or the act performed. What we experienced becomes recollected anew, and thought in terms that could not have been thought at the time." Ian Hacking, *The Social Construction of What?* (Harvard University Press, 1999), 130.

8. Hacking, "Looping Effects of Human Kinds," 375–76.

9. Hacking, "How 'Natural' Are 'Kinds' of Sexual Orientation?," 105.

10. Hacking, "Looping Effects of Human Kinds," 380.
11. Hacking, "Looping Effects of Human Kinds," 381.
12. According to Jordan Redman, "Today, gay is a socially acceptable term for homosexual people. However, this word is rooted in the classification of certain types of people as illicit, countercultural or behaving in ways that go against the respectable conventions of society." Redman, "The History of the Word 'Gay,'" *Gayly*, June 17, 2018, https://www.gayly.com/history-word-%E2%80%9Cgay%E2%80%9D.
13. Daven Hiskey, "How 'Gay' Came to Mean 'Homosexual,'" *Today I Found Out*, February 25, 2010, https://www.todayifoundout.com/index.php/2010/02/how-gay-came-to-mean-homosexual.
14. Mollie Clarke, "'Queer' History: A History of Queer," The National Archives (UK), February 9, 2021, https://blog.nationalarchives.gov.uk/queer-history-a-history-of-queer.
15. Clarke, "'Queer' History."
16. Clarke, "'Queer' History."
17. Hacking, "Making Up People," in *Reconstructing Individualism*, 227.
18. Hacking, "Making Up People," in *Reconstructing Individualism*, 227.
19. Hacking, "Making Up People," in *Reconstructing Individualism*, 228.
20. Ian Hacking, "Autistic Autobiography," *Philosophical Transactions of the Royal Society of London* 364, no. 1522 (2009): 1467.
21. Hacking, "Autistic Autobiography," 1467.
22. Cover, *Identity and Digital Communication*; Cover, *Emergent Identities*, 64–72.
23. Cover, *Emergent Identities*, 64–65.
24. "The Trevor Project National Survey on LGBTQ Youth Mental Health 2019," The Trevor Project, 2019, https://www.thetrevorproject.org/wp-content/uploads/2019/06/The-Trevor-Project-National-Survey-Results-2019.pdf.
25. Douwe Draaisma, "Stereotypes of Autism," *Philosophical Transactions of the Royal Society of London* 364, no. 1522 (2009): 1476.
26. Mark A. Yarhouse, Janet Dean, Stephen P. Stratton, and Julia Sadusky, "Micro-Minoritized and Emerging Sexual and Gender Identities," symposium conducted at the Christian Association for Psychological Studies national conference, Atlanta, GA, March 22, 2024.
27. Hacking, "Looping Effects of Human Kinds," 382.

Chapter 4 Controversies in Ministry

1. Rob Cover, *Emergent Identities: New Sexualities, Genders and Relationships in a Digital Age* (Routledge, 2019), 25–28.
2. Stanton L. Jones and Mark A. Yarhouse, "A Longitudinal Study of Attempted Religiously-Mediated Sexual Orientation Change," *Journal of Sex and Marital Therapy* 37 (2011): 404–27. As I (Mark) looked at the longitudinal data we collected, it struck me that while there may have been some underlying shifts in attraction or even orientation for some participants, the most significant changes reported by participants were in the first year of ministry involvement. Those changes were maintained over the next four to five years, but there was not typically

an increase in change over time. This was inconsistent with the expectation that orientation change would be a gradual shift over several years. Rather, what seems more likely to change in that first year of ministry is *behavior* (they were entering a ministry and often discontinued sexual behavior that was problematic for them) and *identity* (they were instructed by the ministry leaders not to refer to themselves as "gay" but to use more descriptive language, as when a person says, "I experience same-sex attraction" or "I experience SSA").

3. Greg Johnson, *Still Time to Care: What We Can Learn from the Church's Failed Attempt to Cure Homosexuality* (Zondervan, 2021), 85.

4. Lisa M. Diamond, *Sexual Fluidity: Understanding Women's Love and Desire* (Harvard University Press, 2009), 161–63.

5. To be clear, we are not asserting that our Christian beliefs about marriage and sexual ethics are incorrect because they reflect a residual taxonomy; rather, we believe the truth of Christian doctrine exists independent of whether it is communicated in residual terms or in the newer frameworks of our broader society. However, we do believe that the prevalence of sexual orientation change efforts in some Christian ministries is a reflection of the residual framework rather than an inherent truth in Christian doctrines of marriage and sexual ethics. As such, we believe Christians can remain faithful to biblical teaching without continuing to promote sexual orientation change efforts.

6. We know of a nonnegligible group of people who enter into mixed-orientation marriages, or marriages where one spouse experiences a sexual minority orientation. We are not saying that this is never feasible or sustainable but are also not commending it as the expected outcome for all or most sexual minority youth. There are challenges and opportunities within any marriage, and mixed-orientation marriages are no exception. While God may invite some sexual minorities to marry heterosexually, we are cautioning against the approach that assumes this path for many people, which sometimes has been encouraged without robust discernment of individual callings.

7. What we refer to here as models for ministry are also approaches to parenting for the Christian. See Mark A. Yarhouse, *Talking to Kids About Gender Identity* (Bethany House, 2023), 10–13.

8. I (Mark) first discussed and developed this concept of ambassadorship in Yarhouse, *Talking to Kids About Gender Identity*, 10–11.

9. I (Mark) introduced these three approaches in Yarhouse, *Understanding Sexual Identity: A Resource for Youth Ministry* (Zondervan, 2013), 169–76.

10. It is worth acknowledging that some people who have made claims of orientation change, specifically claims about sexual temptation completely disappearing as it relates to same-sex attraction, have subsequently disclosed or been discovered to not have spoken truthfully. This, in large part, contributed to the fall of Exodus International's ministry and great mistrust of change approaches in a broader cultural context.

11. Julia A. Sadusky, "Loneliness and the Celibate, Gay Christian" (doctoral dissertation, Regent University, 2019).

12. C. S. Lewis, *Mere Christianity* (Simon & Schuster, 1996), 94. Copyright © 1942, 1943, 1944, 1952 C. S. Lewis Pte. Ltd. Extract reprinted by permission.

13. The same could be said for fasting. Consider how the spiritual discipline of fasting can become problematic if it is done out of a sense of earning God's love or, in the case of people with disordered eating, could be done from a place of self-loathing.

14. Roman Catholic Church, *Catechism of the Catholic Church*, 2nd ed. (United States Catholic Conference, 2000), paragraph 2359.

Chapter 5 A Relational-Narrative Approach to Ministry

1. It's worth acknowledging that the theoretical and philosophical assumptions of narrative therapy approaches come out of postmodern understanding. This is true for nearly every theoretical approach found in modern psychology. We have seen how postmodernism influenced queer theory, and in many ways narrative approaches to counseling and ministry are informed by existentialism, literary criticism (e.g., Jacques Derrida), and French philosophy (e.g., Michel Foucault). See Mark A. Yarhouse and James N. Sells, *Family Therapies: A Comprehensive Christian Appraisal* (IVP Academic, 2017), 264–67. In particular, Foucault's critique of social institutions and the relationship between power and knowledge is present in much of narrative theory. While we could engage critically with narrative theory, we actually find that the relationship to postmodernism could offer helpful points of connection with youth influenced by postmodern understanding.

2. Michael White and David Epston, *Literate Means to Therapeutic Ends* (Dulwich Centre, 1989), 7.

3. The language of "dominant narratives" and "problem stories" comes out of narrative therapy more broadly, and I (Mark) have incorporated this language into my Sexual Identity Therapy model.

4. The way narrative theorists discuss stories is that prevailing stories provide meaning-making significance that influences our behaviors: "The particular story that prevails or dominates in giving meaning to the event of our lives, to a large extent determines the nature of our lived experience and our patterns of actions. When a problem-saturated story predominates, we are repeatedly invited into disappointment and mystery." White and Epston, *Literate Means to Therapeutic Ends*, 7.

5. Thank you to Stephen P. Stratton for making this connection to attachment theory.

6. As we seek to better understand the common chapters of sexual minorities, microminoritized identities that infuse elements of emerging sexual identities (e.g., aromantic) with emerging gender identities (demigirl) will have to be looked at in greater depth. We are drawing on past research that has most often separated sexual identity development and gender identity development, and we have brought them together along with our clinical experience to provide an account of common chapters, but we will continue to gain understanding in future research at the intersection of sexual and gender identity development.

7. We are seeing some shifts in this pattern, at least in clinical spaces, given the emergent sexual identity terrain. For instance, some people may identify as queer even without experiencing same-sex attraction at puberty. It seems that youth are increasingly drawn into LGBTQ+ community affiliation, which means that not

everyone who adopts an emerging sexual identity has necessarily experienced this milestone of sexual attraction.

8. Kevin T. Biondolillo, "Dynamic Journeys: A Narrative Exploration of Sexual Identity Development for Highly Religious, Sexual Minority Emerging Adults in Christian Higher Education" (doctoral dissertation, Wheaton College, 2024), 22.

9. Biondolillo, "Dynamic Journeys," 20.

10. Biondolillo, "Dynamic Journeys," 23.

11. Biondolillo, "Dynamic Journeys," 26.

12. Biondolillo, "Dynamic Journeys," 19.

13. Biondolillo, "Dynamic Journeys," 20.

14. The broader literature on faith and sexual identity suggests four broad outcomes for people navigating these two important aspects of self: (1) reject their sexual identity to maintain their faith identity; (2) reject their faith in order to maintain their sexual identity; (3) compartmentalize their faith and sexual identities; or (4) integrate their faith and sexual identity. Eric M. Rodriguez and Suzanne C. Ouellette, "Gay and Lesbian Christians: Homosexual and Religious Identity Integration in the Members and Participants of a Gay-Positive Church," *Journal for the Scientific Study of Religion* 39, no. 3 (2000): 334. These designations from the broader literature on faith and sexual identity generally map onto the holding patterns we have seen in our line of research. Holding Pattern E is the rejection of either one's faith or one's sexuality. Holding Pattern D is compartmentalizing faith and sexuality. Holding Patterns A, B, and C are all really different ways of integrating faith and sexual identity, very much in keeping with what Rodriguez and Ouellette describe in the broader literature. We might describe these three integrated holding patterns as just variations on the integration of faith and sexual identity.

15. Micaela Cherí Hardyman, "Longitudinal Patterns of Religious/Spiritual and Sexual Identity Integration for Sexual Minority Students on Christian College Campuses" (doctoral dissertation, Wheaton College, 2024).

16. Stephen P. Stratton et al., "Holding Faith and Sexual Identity Together: Sexual Minority Students' Patterns of Holding and Their Related Self-Perceptions, Mental Health, and College Experiences," paper presented at the Christian Association for Psychological Studies national conference, Dallas, TX, March 2019.

17. Stratton et al., "Holding Faith and Sexual Identity Together."

18. Stratton et al., "Holding Faith and Sexual Identity Together."

19. Hardyman, "Longitudinal Patterns."

20. Stratton et al., "Holding Faith and Sexual Identity Together."

21. See Mark A. Yarhouse and Erica S. N. Tan, *Sexual Identity Synthesis: Attributions, Meaning-Making, and the Search for Congruence* (University Press of America, 2004), 108.

22. Hardyman, "Longitudinal Patterns."

23. Hardyman, "Longitudinal Patterns."

24. Thomas Acklin and Boniface Hicks, *Personal Prayer: A Guide for Receiving the Father's Love* (Emmaus Road, 2019), 109.

25. William L. Hathaway et al., "Gender, Sex, Religion and Forms of Life: A Productive Alternative Diversity Paradigm?," workshop conducted at the Christian Association for Psychological Studies national conference, Louisville, KY,

March 30, 2023. The culture wars today are extraordinarily difficult to navigate. This is due, in part, to sexual orientation and gender discordance often being viewed as identities analogous to other forms of diversity such as race. When conceptualized from an essentialist paradigm, sexual orientation and identity are often framed as a primary form of diversity, whereas religion can be presented as a secondary aspect of diversity (ibid.). Religion is a convention; sexuality is a diversity. When conflicts arise, tensions between sexual identity and religious identity often take place on a stage in which one area of diversity—sexual identity—takes precedence as the more fundamental expression of diversity. Reconceptualizing frequent tensions between the religion and sexual diversity areas as differences in Wittgensteinian "forms of life" may offer productive options for pluralistic solutions when navigating these conflicts (ibid.).

26. Indeed, we suspect that all three ministry models with their emphasis on change of orientation, identity, or behavior would ultimately frame their own ministry as based on growth in Christ. They just appear to outsiders and critics as tethering growth in Christ to change of orientation (or identity or behavior), which complicates what it means to grow in Christ in the first place. Also, the deep divide in ministry cultures makes it exceedingly difficult to develop an agreed-upon form of life, since language, culture, and values will not be shared across different ministries.

27. We are aware of examples like Revoice and Eden Invitation as communities anchored in this approach, not with youth but with adult sexual minorities and their support people.

Chapter 6 Narrative Revisited

1. Janet Dean et al., "The Mediating Role of Self-Acceptance in the Psychological Distress of Sexual Minority Students on Christian College Campuses," *Spirituality in Clinical Practice* 8, no. 2 (2021): 132–48.

2. Mark A. Yarhouse, Stephen P. Stratton, and Janet B. Dean, "What We Learned from Listening to Sexual and Gender Minorities," in *Christlike Acceptance Across Deep Difference: Constructive Conversations on Sexuality and Gender*, ed. Ronald W. Pierce and Karen R. Keen (Baker Academic, 2025), 185.

3. Yarhouse, Stratton, and Dean, "What We Learned," 185.

4. Mark A. Yarhouse, *Sexual Identity and Faith: Helping Clients Find Congruence* (Templeton, 2019).

5. We hold this in tension with the need for churches to discern the qualifications for church membership, service, and sacramental preparation. This is outside the scope of our conversation here, but we see this as a real point of challenge for ministry.

Chapter 7 Engaging Youth

1. For application to Catholic ministry settings, it is worth noting that the phrase "sexual identity" is used in church documents to mean a person's identity as male or female. See Roman Catholic Church, *Catechism of the Catholic Church*, 2nd ed. (Libreria Editrice Vaticana, 2012), no. 2333. You may want to adjust your language, then, to "navigating questions of sexual orientation and

faith," so as not to confuse people who understand "sexual identity" to describe maleness and femaleness. At the same time, most youth talk about sexual orientation and identity labels with the term "sexual identity." This is yet another example of how language nuances can complicate ministry terrain and require nimbleness by ministers.

2. This framing of ministry can be found for Catholic readers in Congregation for the Doctrine of the Faith, "Letter to the Bishops of the Catholic Church on the Pastoral Care of Homosexual Persons" (1986), paragraph 16.

3. This data is taken from research that explores the protective and risk factors impacting LGBT youth mental health. See Nerilee Ceatha et al., "Protective Factors for LGBTI+ Youth Wellbeing: A Scoping Review," *International Journal of Environmental Research and Public Health* 18, no. 21 (November 2021): 1–53.

4. Ceatha et al., "Protective Factors for LGBTI+ Youth Wellbeing."

5. This concept of love is drawn from the work of Thomas Aquinas, *Summa Theologiae* I–II, question 26, article 4.

6. For a thoughtful engagement with queer theory that interested youth may be drawn to learning more about, see Abigail Favale, *The Genesis of Gender: A Christian Theory* (Ignatius, 2022). When offering resources to youth, do so with an open hand, by asking the teen, "Would it be helpful to have some titles of books you could check out as you explore this further?"

BIBLIOGRAPHY

Ace Community Survey Team. "2022 Ace Community Survey Summary Report." October 23, 2024. https://acecommunitysurvey.org/2024/10/23/2022-ace-community-survey-summary-report.

Acklin, Thomas, and Boniface Hicks. *Personal Prayer: A Guide for Receiving the Father's Love.* Emmaus Road, 2019.

Ambrosino, Brandon. "The Invention of 'Heterosexuality.'" *BBC*, March 15, 2017. https://bbc.com/future/article/20170315-the-invention-of-heterosexuality.

American Psychiatric Association. *Diagnostic and Statistical Manual of Mental Disorders.* 5th ed. American Psychiatric Association, 2013.

American Psychiatric Association. *Diagnostic and Statistical Manual of Mental Disorders.* 5th ed. Text Revision. American Psychiatric Association, 2022.

Antonsen, Amy N., Bozena Zdaniuk, Morag Yule, and Lori A. Brotto. "Ace and Aro: Understanding Differences in Romantic Attractions Among Persons Identifying as Asexual." *Archives of Sexual Behavior* 49, no. 5 (2020): 1615–30. https://doi.org/10.1007/s10508-019-01600-1.

Bennett, David A. C. *Queering the Queer: An Exploration of How Gay Celibate Asceticism Can Renew and Inform the Role of Desire in Contemporary Anglican Theology.* Doctoral thesis, University of Oxford, 2022.

Bennett, David A. C. "Returning to Spiritual Sense: Cruciform Power and Queer Identities in Analytic Theology." *Religions* 14, no. 12 (2023): 1445–57. https://doi.org/10.3390/rel14121445.

Biondolillo, Kevin T. "Dynamic Journeys: A Narrative Exploration of Sexual Identity Development for Highly Religious, Sexual Minority Emerging Adults in Christian Higher Education." Doctoral dissertation, Wheaton College, 2024.

Blank, Hanne. *Straight: The Surprisingly Short History of Heterosexuality*. Beacon, 2012.

Busse, Heide, Tara Harrop, David Gunnell, and Ruth Kipping. "Prevalence and Associated Harm of Engagement in Self-Asphyxial Behaviours ('Choking Game') in Young People: A Systematic Review." *Archives of Disease in Childhood* 100, no. 12 (2015). https://pmc.ncbi.nlm.nih.gov/articles/PMC4680200.

Butler, Judith. "Performative Acts and Gender Constitution: An Essay in Phenomenology and Feminist Theory." In *Performing Feminisms: Feminist Critical Theory and Theatre*, edited by Sue-Ellen Case. Johns Hopkins University Press, 1990.

Carvalho, Ana C., and David L. Rodrigues. "Sexuality, Sexual Behavior, and Relationships of Asexual Individuals: Differences Between Aromantic and Romantic Orientation." *Archives of Sexual Behavior* 51, no. 4 (2022): 2159–68. https://doi.org/10.1007/s10508-021-02187-2.

Ceatha, Nerilee, Aaron C. C. Koay, Conor Buggy, Oscar James, Louise Tully, Marta Bustillo, and Des Crowley. "Protective Factors for LGBTI+ Youth Wellbeing: A Scoping Review." *International Journal of Environmental Research and Public Health* 18, no. 21 (November 2021): 1–53.

Chesterton, G. K. *G. K. Chesterton: The Autobiography of G. K. Chesterton*. Ignatius, 2006.

Clarke, Mollie. "'Queer' History: A History of Queer." The National Archives (UK), February 9, 2021. https://blog.nationalarchives.gov.uk/queer-history-a-history-of-queer.

Copulsky, Daniel, and Phillip L. Hammack. "Asexuality, Graysexuality, and Demisexuality: Distinctions in Desire, Behavior, and Identity." *Journal of Sex Research* 60, no. 2 (2023): 221–30. https://doi.org/10.1080/00224499.2021.2012113.

Cover, Rob. *Emergent Identities: New Sexualities, Genders and Relationships in a Digital Age*. Routledge, 2019.

Cover, Rob. *Identity and Digital Communication: Concepts, Theories, Practices*. Routledge, 2023.

de Lauretis, Teresa. "Queer Theory: Lesbian and Gay Sexualities: An Introduction." *differences* 3, no. 2 (Summer 1991): iii–xviii.

Dean, Janet, Stephen P. Stratton, and Mark A. Yarhouse. "The Mediating Role of Self-Acceptance in the Psychological Distress of Sexual Minority Students on Christian College Campuses." *Spirituality in Clinical Practice* 8, no. 2 (2021): 132–48. https://doi.org/10.1037/scp0000253.

Diamond, Lisa M. *Sexual Fluidity: Understanding Women's Love and Desire*. Harvard University Press, 2009.

Draaisma, Douwe. "Stereotypes of Autism." *Philosophical Transactions of the Royal Society of London* 364, no. 1522 (2009): 1475–80. https://doi.org/10.1098/rstb.2008.0324.

Favale, Abigail. *The Genesis of Gender: A Christian Theory*. Ignatius, 2022.

Foucault, Michel. *Power/Knowledge: Selected Interviews and Other Writings, 1972–1977*. Edited by Colin Gordon. Pantheon, 1980.

Francis, Pope. *Amoris Laetitia*. March 19, 2016. https://www.vatican.va/content/dam/francesco/pdf/apost_exhortations/documents/papa-francesco_esortazione-ap_20160319_amoris-laetitia_en.pdf.

Hacking, Ian. "Autistic Autobiography." *Philosophical Transactions of the Royal Society of London* 364, no. 1522 (2009): 1467–73. https://doi.org/10.1098/rstb.2008.0329.

Hacking, Ian. "How 'Natural' Are 'Kinds' of Sexual Orientation?" *Law and Philosophy* 12, no. 1 (2002): 95–107.

Hacking, Ian. "The Looping Effects of Human Kinds." In *Causal Cognition: An Interdisciplinary Approach*, edited by Dan Sperber, David Premack, and Ann James Premack, 351–83. Oxford University Press, 1995.

Hacking, Ian. "Making Up People." In *Reconstructing Individualism: Autonomy, Individuality, and the Self in Western Thought*, edited by Thomas C. Heller, Morton Sosna, and David E. Wellbery, 222–36. Stanford University Press, 1986.

Hacking, Ian. "Making Up People." *London Review of Books* 28, no. 16 (2006): 23–26. https://www.lrb.co.uk/v28/n16/ian-hacking/making-up-people.

Hacking, Ian. *The Social Construction of What?* Harvard University Press, 1999.

Halperin, D. M. *Saint Foucault: Toward a Gay Hagiography*. Oxford University Press, 1995.

Hardyman, Micaela Cherí. "Longitudinal Patterns of Religious/Spiritual and Sexual Identity Integration for Sexual Minority Students on Christian College Campuses." Doctoral dissertation, Wheaton College, 2024.

Haslam, N. "Looping Effects and the Expanding Concept of Mental Disorder." *Journal of Psychopathology* 22, no. 4 (2016): 4–9.

Hathaway, William L., and Mark A. Yarhouse. *The Integration of Psychology and Christianity: A Domain-Based Approach*. IVP Academic, 2021.

Hathaway, William L., Mark A. Yarhouse, Stephen P. Stratton, and Janet B. Dean. "Gender, Sex, Religion and Forms of Life: A Productive Alternative Diversity Paradigm?" Workshop conducted at the Christian Association for Psychological Studies national conference, Louisville, KY, March 30, 2023.

Hille, Jessica J. "Beyond Sex: A Review of Recent Literature on Asexuality." *Current Opinion in Psychology* 49 (2023). https://doi.org/10.1016/j.copsyc.2022.101516.

Hiskey, Daven. "How 'Gay' Came to Mean 'Homosexual.'" *Today I Found Out*, February 25, 2010. https://www.todayifoundout.com/index.php/2010/02/how-gay-came-to-mean-homosexual.

Huijer, Marli. "A Critical Use of Foucault's Art of Living." *Foundations of Science* 22 (2017): 323–27. https://doi.org/10.1007/s10699-015-9441-z.

Johnson, Greg. *Still Time to Care: What We Can Learn from the Church's Failed Attempt to Cure Homosexuality*. Zondervan, 2021.

Johnson, Jay Emerson. *Peculiar Faith: Queer Theology for Christian Witness*. Seabury, 2014.

Jones, Stanton L., and Mark A. Yarhouse. "A Longitudinal Study of Attempted Religiously-Mediated Sexual Orientation Change." *Journal of Sex and Marital Therapy* 37 (2011): 404–27. https://doi.org/10.1080/0092623X.2011.607052.

Kalafatis-Russell, Angel Renee. "Doing Kink vs. Being Kinky: A Systematic Scoping Review of the Literature on BDSM Behavior, Orientation, and Identity." Master's thesis, University of North Florida, 2021. https://digitalcommons.unf.edu/etd/1108.

Katz, Jonathan Ned. *The Invention of Heterosexuality*. Dutton, 1995.

Lewis, C. S. *Mere Christianity*. Simon & Schuster, 1996.

McQuillan, Susan. "The Many Shades of Asexuality: Graysexuality, Quoisexuality, Apothisexuality, and More." *Psychology Today*, January 15, 2024. https://www.psychologytoday.com/us/blog/cravings/202401/asexuality-demisexuality-graysexuality-and-more.

Nichols, Margaret, and James P. Fedor. "Treating Sexual Problems in Clients Who Practice 'Kink.'" In *The Wiley Handbook of Sex Therapy*, edited by Zoë D. Peterson, 420–34. Wiley & Sons, 2017.

Patterson, Daniel R. *Reforming a Theology of Gender: Constructive Reflections on Judith Butler and Queer Theory*. Cascade Books, 2022.

Rodriguez, Eric M., and Suzanne C. Ouellette. "Gay and Lesbian Christians: Homosexual and Religious Identity Integration in the Members and Participants of a Gay-Positive Church." *Journal for the Scientific Study of Religion* 39, no. 3 (2000): 333–47. https://doi.org/10.1111/0021-8294.00028.

Roman Catholic Church. *Catechism of the Catholic Church*. 2nd ed. United States Catholic Conference, 2000.

Sabia-Tanis, Justin. "Holy Creation, Wholly Creative: God's Intention for Gender Diversity." In *Understanding Transgender Identities: Four Views*, edited by James K. Beilby and Paul Rhodes Eddy, 195–222. Baker Academic, 2019.

Sadusky, Julia A. "Loneliness and the Celibate, Gay Christian." Doctoral dissertation, Regent University, 2019.

Smith, James K. A. *Imagining the Kingdom: How Worship Works*. Baker Academic, 2013.

Stratton, Stephen P., Janet B. Dean, and Mark A. Yarhouse. "Holding Faith and Sexual Identity Together: Sexual Minority Students' Patterns of Holding and Their Related Self-Perceptions, Mental Health, and College Experiences." Paper presented at the Christian Association for Psychological Studies national conference, Dallas, TX, March 2019.

Taylor, Charles. *A Secular Age*. Harvard University Press, 2007.

Tonstad, Linn Marie. "Ambivalent Loves: Christian Theologies, Queer Theologies." *Literature and Theology* 31, no. 4 (2017): 472–89. https://doi.org/10.1093/litthe/frw043.

Tonstad, Linn Marie. *God and Difference: The Trinity, Sexuality, and the Transformation of Finitude*. Routledge, 2016.

White, Michael, and David Epston. *Literate Means to Therapeutic Ends*. Dulwich Centre, 1989.

Williams, Raymond. *Marxism and Literature*. Oxford University Press, 1977.

Wittgenstein, Ludwig. *Philosophical Investigations*. Edited by G. E. M. Anscombe. Wiley-Blackwell, 1953.

Yarhouse, Mark A. *Sexual Identity and Faith: Helping Clients Find Congruence*. Templeton, 2019.

Yarhouse, Mark A. *Talking to Kids About Gender Identity*. Bethany House, 2023.

Yarhouse, Mark A. *Understanding Sexual Identity: A Resource for Youth Ministry*. Zondervan, 2013.

Yarhouse, Mark A., Janet B. Dean, Stephen P. Stratton, and Julia A. Sadusky. "Micro-Minoritized and Emerging Sexual and Gender Identities." Symposium conducted at the Christian Association for Psychological Studies national conference, Atlanta, GA, March 22, 2024.

Yarhouse, Mark A., and Julia Sadusky. *Emerging Gender Identities: Understanding the Diverse Experiences of Today's Youth*. Brazos, 2022.

Yarhouse, Mark A., and James N. Sells. *Family Therapies: A Comprehensive Christian Appraisal*. IVP Academic, 2017.

Yarhouse, Mark A., Stephen P. Stratton, and Janet B. Dean. "What We Learned from Listening to Sexual and Gender Minorities." In *Christlike Acceptance Across Deep Difference: Constructive Conversations on Sexuality and Gender*, edited by Ronald W. Pierce and Karen R. Keen, 177–90. Baker Academic, 2025.

Yarhouse, Mark A., and Erica S. N. Tan. *Sexual Identity Synthesis: Attributions, Meaning-Making, and the Search for Congruence*. University Press of America, 2004.

Yarhouse, Mark A., and Olya Zaporozhets. *Costly Obedience: What We Can Learn from the Celibate Gay Christian Community*. Zondervan, 2019.

INDEX

ace spectrum, 4, 21, 25–27, 33, 69, 86
ambassador, 109–11, 142, 166–67, 176, 192, 197
androsexual, 4, 9, 92
aroace, 4
aromantic, 4, 21, 26–27, 113, 123, 186
asexual, 3–5, 9, 21, 25–27, 36, 82, 86, 94, 120, 136, 157, 172, 179, 186

BDSM (bondage, discipline, sadism, masochism), 33–34
biromantic, 5, 26–27, 82, 84, 103, 148, 160
bisexual, xiii, 5–6, 8–9, 12–13, 16, 20–21, 27, 42, 79, 82–83, 85, 88, 103, 135, 147, 159
Butler, Judith, 51, 54, 64, 205n7

celibacy, 50, 105, 116–17
conversion therapies, 13–14
counternarrative, 126–27, 129, 162
Cover, Rob, 10, 23, 35, 53, 83
cupiosexual, 5, 8, 26, 103

de Lauretis, Teresa, 42–43
demiromantic, 5, 9, 27

demisexual, xiii, 5, 8–9, 20, 26–27
Diamond, Lisa, 16–17
discipleship, 116, 119, 166, 187–88, 192–94
disclosure, 56–58, 124, 147, 155–58, 172, 178, 181
dominant taxonomy, xiii, 9, 12, 15, 18–21, 31, 36, 42, 77, 79, 81, 94, 109, 126, 168, 193
typology, 82
dynamic nominalism, 82

emergent taxonomy, 17–20, 22, 36, 65, 92, 94–95, 98, 99, 102–3, 110, 148, 152, 168, 175, 197
identities, 29
empathic receptivity, 156

form of life, 141–43, 190, 193, 195
Foucault, Michel, 42–43, 47, 49, 59–60

gay, history of term, 76–78
grace for self, 156–57
grayromantic, 5, 27
graysexual, 5, 9, 20–21, 27, 82, 103, 165

Hacking, Ian, 66, 69–73, 75–78, 80–82, 85, 87
Halperin, David, 56–57
heteroflexible, 5
heterosexuality, 12, 42–43, 46–48, 54, 58–59, 61, 78, 80, 102, 111, 181
  history of, 29–32
homosexuality, 45, 48, 58, 61, 75–77, 80–81, 83, 85–86, 91, 96, 98–99, 112, 152, 166
  homosexual, 8, 11–12, 14–15, 18, 20, 30–32, 35, 46, 70, 77–79, 93, 98, 103, 111, 114
  homosexual orientation, 14, 44

identity, private and public, 6, 71, 135

Johnson, Greg, 97
Johnson, Jay, 60–61, 63

Kertbeny, Karl, 30–31
kink, 33–34

lesbian, xiii, 5–6, 8–9, 12–13, 16, 20–21, 23, 32, 42–45, 50, 69, 79–80, 82–83, 85, 88, 94, 98, 103
Lewis, C. S., 118
looping effect, 66, 69–72, 74–75, 78–85, 86, 115, 132, 175–76, 191, 195

microminoritized identities, 9, 87, 95

nominalists, 80
nonmonogamy, 33

omnisexual, xiii, 5
  omnisexuality, 6, 33

panromantic, 5, 26
pansexual, 5, 9, 113
  pansexuality, 6, 33

polysexual, 6
pomosexual, 6, 20, 103
  pomosexuality, 33

queer, 6, 26, 60–61, 65, 76, 88, 94, 103, 113, 124, 129, 147, 157, 160, 162, 165, 179–80
  history of term, 77–78
  theology, 61–65
  theorists, 32, 48–49, 52, 54, 56, 58
  theory, xiv, 37, 39–60, 65–66, 92, 108–9, 121, 143, 188, 190–93, 195

realists, 80
residual taxonomy, 10, 20, 92–95, 97–98, 102–3, 107, 122, 158, 172–73, 194

Sedgwick, Eve Kosofsky, 43, 56
sexual attraction, xiii, 5–6, 16–17, 21, 25–26, 31, 92, 101, 103, 106, 113, 115, 121, 148, 152, 157, 172, 179–80, 189
sexual orientation change efforts, 13–14, 96, 98, 102
shame, 57–58, 92, 101, 107, 128–31, 143, 148, 150–51
sides in the gay Christian discussion, 88, 105–6, 111, 114, 158
skoliosexual, 6, 8
Smith, James K. A., 52
social media, 23, 52–54
spectrasexual, 6, 8
Storkey, Elaine, 58

Trevor Project, The, 8, 25, 83–84

Victorian, 11, 20

Wittgenstein, Ludwig, 141

MARK YARHOUSE (PsyD, Wheaton College), a licensed clinical psychologist, is the Dr. Arthur P. Rech and Mrs. Jean May Rech Professor of Psychology in the School of Psychology, Counseling, and Family Therapy at Wheaton College in Wheaton, Illinois, where he directs the Sexual and Gender Identity Institute. Yarhouse has authored or coauthored several books, including the well-received *Understanding Gender Dysphoria*.

Connect with Dr. Yarhouse:

www.markyarhouse.com

 @markyarhouse

JULIA SADUSKY (PsyD, Regent University) works as a clinical psychologist in Denver, Colorado. She also serves as a youth and ministry educator, offering trainings and consultations on the intersection of sexuality, gender, and theology. Her research experiences and clinical training have focused on the study of sexual and gender identity, including providing individual, family, couples, and group therapy for those navigating sexual- and gender-identity concerns. She is an adviser for the Center for Faith, Sexuality and Gender.

Connect with Dr. Sadusky:

www.juliasadusky.com

 drsadusky   @drsadusky

www.ingramcontent.com/pod-product-compliance
Lightning Source LLC
Chambersburg PA
CBHW020229170426
43201CB00007B/364